Praise for *501 Ways to Roll Out the Red Carpet for Your Customers*

"Nothing is more powerful than people who know how to roll out the red carpet for their customers. Donna Cutting writes with passion about innovative ways service providers give a world-class experience to their customers. Put the ideas in this book into action and you'll fascinate your customers with red carpet service."
—Sally Hogshead, author of *How the World Sees You*

"In today's economy customer service is your competitive advantage; how you get above the white noise to attract new customers, and how you add value to retain the great customers you have. However, understand how to provide that exceptional service, and how to get your entire team to engaged to implement these out of the box ideas can be a constant challenge. Now, Donna Cutting has written the book that not only makes this process easy, she has written the book that will spark the innovative thinking and ownership you need to get every member of your team motivated to deliver exceptional service to every customer every time! In this fun and entertaining read, Donna has gone to the experts, found not only amazing customer service stories, but she found (and is sharing) stories and ideas that work! You are going to love this read, you are going to want to read it as a team, and you are going to want to keep it on your shelf as resource and the perfect onboarding tool!"
—Meridith Elliott Powell, Business Growth Expert, author of *Winning In The Trust and Value Economy, and Own It*

"Donna Cutting's book is a time saver for anyone who wants to provide red carpet customer service. She's compiled 501-ready-to-execute strategies for treating your customers (both internal and external) like royalty. There's nothing more productive than having happy customers, and this book will help you get there quickly!"
—Laura Stack, The Productivity Pro® and author of *Doing the Right Things Right*

"Donna Cutting's first book, *The Celebrity Experience*, is a favorite of mine. I have called it the Bible of customer service and recommended it to all of our clients. However, with *501 Ways to Roll Out the Red Carpet for Your Customers*, Donna has not only done it again, she's topped herself. You could almost start reading on any page and find a practical idea for delivering extraordinary service to your customers (and employees!) However, I recommend you start at the beginning. This is a fun-to-read, feel-good book that will not only spark your own creative juices, but will have you laughing and crying to boot. Buy your own copy - and then buy copies for everyone on your team."

—Traci Bild, Founder & CEO of Bild & Company, and author of *Get Your Girl Back*

"It takes happy, engaged employees to create delighted customers. In her book, *501 Ways to Roll Out the Red Carpet for Your Customers*, Donna Cutting offers practical advice for leaders who want to create an entire culture of service excellence. From tips on how to hire service professionals, to keeping employees focused on your mission, to making red carpet first and last impressions, there are ideas in here for everyone who wants to turn employees and customers into advocates for their business."

—Richard Hadden, author of *Contented Cows Still Give Better Milk*

501 WAYS TO

ROLL OUT

THE RED CARPET

FOR YOUR

CUSTOMERS

EASY-TO-IMPLEMENT IDEAS TO
INSPIRE LOYALTY, GET NEW CUSTOMERS,
AND LEAVE A LASTING IMPRESSION

DONNA CUTTING

501 WAYS TO ROLL OUT THE RED CARPET FOR CUSTOMERS
EDITED BY KIRSTEN DALLEY
TYPESET BY KRISTIN GOBLE
Cover design by Ty Nowicki
Printed in the U.S.A.

Image on page 21 courtesy of Durham Performing Arts Center; image on page 65 courtesy of Hospice of Marshall County; image on page 102 courtesy of Northwell Health, formerly North Shore LIJ; image on page 117 courtesy of Debbie Ley; image on page 126 courtesy of Salmeron Financial; image on page 189 courtesy of G Adventures; image on page 193 courtesy of Ruby Receptionists.

The Ruby Service Pyramid is a registered trademark of Ruby Receptionists.
The Net Promoter Score is a registered trademark of Richard Owen, Laura Brooks, and Fred Reichheld.
Director of WOW! is a registered trademark of High Point University
DaVinci Office Solutions is a registered trademark or DaVinci Virtual Office Solutions.
VideoDorsements is a registered trademark of Celebrity Source.
Fan Braggin' is a registered trademark of The Experience Pros.

To order this title, please call toll-free 1-800-CAREER-1 (NJ and Canada: 201-848-0310) to order using VISA or MasterCard, or for further information on books from Career Press.

The Career Press, Inc.
12 Parish Drive
Wayne, NJ 07470
www.careerpress.com

Library of Congress Cataloging-in-Publication Data
CIP Data Available Upon Request.

This book is dedicated to Connor McCray and Noah McCray, funny, talented, wonderful young men; Katharina Boyd Carter, a brave, beautiful young woman; and Keiran, Soren, and Eliana.

A portion of the proceeds from this book will be donated to the Lollipop Theater: *www.lollipoptheater.com.*

I'd like to thank...

Each and every year I watch the Academy Awards. To this day, I still dream about what I might say if I were the recipient of that coveted award. When I was a child I would practice my speech in the mirror, talking into my hairbrush. Today, I review it in my head—a far more dignified approach for a grown adult. Oh, who am I kidding? Sometimes I still get the old hairbrush out! What I've learned over the years from watching is that it takes a village to create an artist, make a movie, and get someone to the point where he or she is on that stage.

The same might be said of writing a book. There is absolutely no way I could thank every single person who supported me in some way during this journey. I will try to thank each of you individually and in person. However, there are a few people I'd like to acknowledge here on this stage—I mean, page:

Jim Cutting—you are the love of my life. Thank you for loving this crazy artist. You and me.

Rachel Street, Director of Delight—I seriously could not have done this without you. You live up to your title every single day!

Lisa Hagan—the *best* agent I could ever imagine. How did I get so lucky?

Gail Lennon—editor and proofreader extraordinaire.

Ellen Winner—for doing so much wonderful research.

Kyle Spencer—master of transcription and tight deadlines. You are awesome.

Brandi Hand, Tia Robinson, Laura Neff, Dani Fake, Laurel Scherer, Nick Romanos, and Meridith Elliott-Powell—for your various contributions to the book and the brand.

Adam Schwartz, Kirsten Dalley, Laurie Kelly-Pye, and the entire team at Career Press—what an absolute pleasure it is to work with you.

Cydney Koukol—for all the great introductions. I'm your fan!

Peter Shankman—for starting HARO.

My wonderful customers, family, friends and members of the National Speakers Association—I'm incredibly blessed to work with you, play with you, and learn with you!

Every single person who responded to my queries and shared his or her story with me for this book—I'm incredibly proud to share your red-carpet examples with my readers and audiences!

And finally, Moxie and Tonks—for making us laugh every single day, even in the midst of deadlines!

CONTENTS

CHAPTER ONE

Coming Attractions

You have an awesome responsibility.

If you picked up this book, chances are you are in some way responsible for ensuring that your customers have an extraordinary experience. Perhaps you're a mid-level manager at a large company, trying to get your team members to deliver consistently excellent customer service. Perhaps you're the administrator of a healthcare facility or the general manager of a hotel, looking for ways to delight your patients or guests. Or maybe you're an entrepreneur trying to differentiate yourself from the competition.

Whatever your job, it should come as no surprise to you that providing an outstanding experience for your customers is critical to the survival of your organization. Not only do today's customers have more choices than ever, but thanks to social media, they also have a more influential voice than ever before. As my friend Charles McIntyre would say, "It's no longer word of mouth; it's world of mouth."

This may be one of the reasons you chose to buy a book about customer service.

Before we go any further, let me explain what red-carpet customer service means to me. When I was a young girl growing up in

Westport, Massachusetts, we would often visit my French grandparents, who we called Memère and Pepère. They had 14 children, so as you can imagine, we had a *very* large family. (That was just on Dad's side of the family!)

One day, when Memère and Pepère were coming back from a trip, my mom found a long remnant of a red carpet and rolled it out to greet them upon their arrival. Subsequently, my memère used it to welcome family members who lived out of state and were coming home to visit. I excitedly watched from the window and felt it was similar to treating our loved ones as if they were stars of the silver screen!

This is the essence my red-carpet brand. To me, when you roll out the red carpet for your customers, you're treating them as if they're important and special, like treasured friends or members of your family. When you do this consistently, your customers can't help but give you rave reviews and repeat business.

The fact is, there has never been a better time to focus on rolling out the red carpet for your customers. A study by Harris Interactive in 2011 determined that 89 percent of consumers quit doing business with a company (and went to a competitor) because of a bad customer experience (source: *Customer Experience Impact Report* by Harris Interactive/ Right Now, 2011). Compare this to 59 percent in 2007 and you'll see that one of two things is happening: Either customer service has gotten worse; or consumers, armed with more choices, are becoming more empowered. Perhaps both are true.

Given this, it shouldn't shock you to know that news of a bad customer experience reaches more than twice as many ears as praise for a good service experience (source: White House Office of Consumer Affairs report, from *www.helpscout.net/75-customer-service-facts -quotes-statistics/*.) However, when you blow your customer away with both excellent service *and* what I call "movie moments," the good news can also go viral. In fact, 55 percent of consumers are willing to recommend a company due to outstanding service over product or price (source: *Customer Experience Impact Report* by Harris Interactive/Right Now, 2010).

Consider all the time, money, and resources that go into marketing and sales for your business. What if you spent a fraction of that ensuring you don't blow the potential for repeat business and referrals by delivering a poor customer experience? Did you know it's six or seven times more expensive to acquire a new customer than it is to keep a current one (source: White House Office of Consumer Affairs report)?

There's a direct link between service and sales. The real sale is made *after* you earn the customer. You may have crackerjack salespeople who bring in new customers right and left. If you do, bravo! Now's the time for you to decide: Is it uphill or downhill from there? As Don Draper in *Mad Men* put it, "The day you sign a client is the day you start losing one."

If you picked up this book, though, you probably already know these things. More than likely, you're like me. You're ready and raring to provide the highest level of service to your customers. You get jazzed about treating your clients as if they were stars. You're itching to make memorable moments that spread like wildfire.

The problem is, who has the time?

If you're like most people, you have 50 million things on your to-do list. Coming up with creative ways to roll out the red carpet for customers sometimes takes a back seat. Or perhaps you've heard that the best employee and customer experiences start at the top, and you're a mid-level manager. Or maybe you're a small business owner with champagne dreams and a beer budget.

If any of those scenarios sound familiar, this book has something for you!

How can you be expected to design an extraordinary customer experience when you have too much to do? Or too few resources? Or when you're on information and technology overload? Or when every time slot in your day is already scheduled for you by the very people at corporate who want you to be creative? The good news is that you don't have to reinvent the wheel. There are people in organizations of all sizes who have imagined and implemented fantastic ideas that have surprised and delighted their customers. They and I are generously sharing 501 of them here for your adoption and inspiration!

Does an extraordinary employee and customer experience start at the top? Is it more than one manager can do on his or her own? The answer to both questions is yes. Revolutionizing the entire customer experience takes planning and commitment. It takes a strong vision that excites and ignites your team. It takes hiring the right people, then engaging, empowering, and encouraging them. It takes 100-percent accountability and a definite decision that you are going to raise the bar. Sometimes it's fun and sometimes it's not.

However, regardless of who you are or what your title is, you can take small actions that make a big impact. Sometimes it takes someone like you to get the process started. *501 Ways to Roll Out the Red Carpet for Your Customers* offers you a long list of service improvements you can make in bite-sized chunks that are easy to swallow. Each check mark, number, and bullet in the text denotes an idea that has worked for me or others, and can work for you, too. Keep reading! You'll also find some great examples of hiring strategies, employee engagement techniques, and other ideas for laying the foundation for a total red-carpet experience, inside and outside your company.

Budget tight? You'll find it doesn't always take a million dollars to make a million-dollar impact. The ideas shared in *501 Ways to Roll Out the Red Carpet for Your Customers* fit a wide variety of budgets and come from organizations of all sizes and types. They come from large corporations, small and large senior living organizations, healthcare facilities, performing arts centers, realtors, solo entrepreneurs, small independent restaurants, regional theatres, colleges and universities, hotels, receptionist services, cinema chains, and solo tradespeople. If you work in a service industry of any kind, chances are you are represented here.

But remember: The way to innovate *inside* your industry is to look *outside* your industry for inspiration. Some of your best red-carpet successes will come from ideas you borrowed from outside your field and then adapted, to the surprise and delight of *your* customers.

You'll read about a cinema chain that found a unique way to use storytelling and community involvement to teach their staff members about customer service.

You'll learn from a service excellence manager at a hospital who found a way to bring hospitality to the emergency room.

You'll enjoy the story of a financial advisor who wows his clients by helping them beat the heat.

You'll be delighted by the consultants who literally roll out the red carpet for guests visiting their office.

You'll read about a restaurant where people go because they look forward to experiencing the wait!

You'll meet both a "mayor" and a "culture fairy"!

You'll learn about a city that rolls out the red carpet rather than the red tape.

You may even have a celebrity sighting or two.

I could go on and on about the cool people and innovative ideas within these pages, but I'll let you discover them for yourself.

Ideally, this is a book you'll mark up with a pencil, sticky notes, or a digital highlighter. Read through *501 Ways to Roll Out the Red Carpet for Your Customers* once. Make notes about the ideas that excite you and the stories that hit you emotionally. If you're working with a team, discuss these ideas with them (preferably after providing the members of your team with their own copies). Review and answer the questions for discussion at the end of each chapter. Choose one or two ideas that you'll implement immediately. Be sure to celebrate your results! Then, repeat with a new idea.

This brings me to the impetus for writing this book. In my first book, *The Celebrity Experience: Insider Secrets to Delivering Red-Carpet Customer Service*, I asked readers to imagine what it would be like if they treated their customers like stars. I interviewed people who serve celebrities. I talked to them about what it takes to deliver true red-carpet service to those who've come to expect it. Some of the most fascinating stories, however, came from people in organizations that are creating a daily, extraordinary experiences for ordinary folks like you and me. One of those featured organizations was High Point University.

The mission of High Point University (HPU) is that every student receives an extraordinary education in an inspiring environment surrounded by caring people. The HPU focus is on academic excellence. At the same time, they have managed to create one of the most unique, red-carpet student experiences ever. As a result, they have tripled their freshman class in less than 10 years. They've increased the size of their campus and offerings. They've won countless awards, including being named number one in the "America's Best Colleges" list published by *U.S. News and World Report* and number four in private university "return on investment."

One of the ideas shared by the leadership team of High Point University was their welcome sign. When a prospective student or special guest is expected, he or she is directed to park in a space marked with a welcome sign personalized with his or her name. It's a big *wow*. Many stop to pose for a photo with the sign before heading inside for an appointment.

After *The Celebrity Experience* was released, I began to notice a common theme in my travels. Wherever I went to deliver a speech, provide training, or meet with customers, there was a welcome sign with my name on it. Sometimes it was at a parking space; other times it was perched on a reception desk. The signs weren't just for me, though. Often, my customers would say, "We now welcome each guest or prospective client with a personalized sign. We learned it from your book."

I can't tell you how fabulous it feels when you share ideas, and people implement them! Readers embraced and exemplified many other stories from *The Celebrity Experience,* but the personalized sign seems to be the one that *everyone* implemented.

I mentioned this to my friend Nido Qubein, the president of High Point University and the person who is largely responsible for leading the university's transformation. He looked at me thoughtfully and said, "You know, I think what we did well is string a whole lot of those little ideas together." It's true. Visit HPU and you'll spend a lot of time with your jaw on the floor. It's one *wow* moment after another.

After that conversation, the idea for the book you're holding in your hands began to form. What if I could share hundreds of actionable tactics that my readers could string together to create their own extraordinary customer experience? *501 Ways to Roll Out the Red Carpet for Your Customers* is my attempt to provide you with 501 of them!

This book is both practical and tactical. You'll discover new ways to:

- Make red-carpet first and last impressions.
- Build a solid foundation and excel at the basics.
- Turn mundane moments into memorable ones.
- Strive for flawless service but recover from gaffes with style.
- Give standing ovations to your staff.
- Use social media, customer events, and community contributions to connect with customers.
- Deliver a "George Clooney–like" experience.
- Turn prospects into customers and customers into raving fans.

One little note about that conversation I had with Dr. Qubein. After we discussed the tactics used at High Point University—some others of which you will read about in this book—he reminded me that the ideas themselves are not enough. You need to have a solid foundation on which to build your extraordinary customer experience. That's why you'll find a chapter in this book titled "Get Red-Carpet Ready." You'll learn about organizational strategies for hiring and onboarding service superstars, training them well, and keeping them inspired to roll out the red carpet for your customers. Finally, you'll be taken through a 30-day plan to get you started on your quest to treat customers like stars.

If there's one thing I've learned in my more than 15 years on the platform, it's that today's audiences need less "why" and more "how-to." *501 Ways to Roll Out the Red Carpet for Your Customers* gives you just that in the form of 501 easy-to-implement ideas for rolling out the red carpet.

Shall we get started? And...*action!*

CHAPTER TWO

Have Them at Hello and Keep Them at Goodbye

When you purchase tickets to see a show at the Durham Performing Arts Center (UPAC), you have high hopes for the particular production you plan to see. What you may not be expecting, though, is the extraordinary experience you will have before *and* after the show.

A couple of years ago, I drove more than three hours from my home in Asheville, North Carolina, to Durham to see a touring production of the Broadway musical *Hair*, which was getting rave reviews. The production and performances were outstanding. Based on the rave reviews from my friends and others, I expected nothing less. However, it was the red-carpet welcome my husband and I (as well as the other guests) received from the staff and volunteers at Durham Performing Arts Center that completely blew me away. In fact, it started before we ever got there and continued well after we arrived home. If you were to see a show at DPAC, here are just a few things they would do to make such a great impression:

✓ Immediately upon purchasing tickets, you receive a confirmation e-mail with a link to details about the event.

✓ Prior to the event, depending on how far ahead you booked your seats, you'll receive several updates with much-needed information about the show. You'll learn everything you need to know, including where to park, where to eat, and even what time you should leave your house based on expected traffic for that day.

✓ You can even preorder your drink so it is ready for you at intermission. Yes, you can take that drink to your seat to sip on during the show!

✓ When you arrive, you'll notice a smiling man or woman (or both) wearing red coats and top hats. They are called DPAC's Showstoppers, and they're standing out front, ready to welcome you. Sometimes, they'll even dance for you. They aren't the only ones, either. As you enter the theater, and make your way across the lobby, and to your seats, uniformed ushers and staff members will greet you with smiles and helpful guidance, all along the way. Everyone honestly seems glad to see you and excited that you're there.

✓ When the show is over, and you make your way through the lobby and back to your car, you'll be greeted with the same enthusiasm. You'll be directed easily to the exit, and sent off with spirited and friendly good-byes and invitations to come back again.

✓ Once home, you'll receive a survey about your experience. If you send it back with comments, Bob Klaus, DPAC's general manager, may personally reply to thank you (as he did for me) or address your concerns.

As the saying goes, you never get a second chance to make a first impression. Traditional wisdom holds that people form their first impression of you within seven seconds. A newer study done by the

University of Glasgow in March 2014, states that it takes a half a second for people to make up their minds about you. In other words, you literally can have them—or not—at "Hello."

The last impression you make may be the one that sticks with your customer the most. The *recency effect*, a psychological term, describes the fact that when asked to recall specific items on a list, people are more likely to first remember those that came at the end of the list. In other words, you can make a smashing first impression and blow it all up with a poor last impression. That's why this chapter focuses on specific examples of how to create a stellar first impression and follow it up with a last impression that will ensure it won't be your customer's last visit.

Let's begin with the beginning, shall we? Here are some terrific ideas that others have put into action to create an amazing arrival experience for their customers.

Splendido's Commencement Day

Once you've decided to move into Splendido, a Mather LifeWays Continuing Care Retirement Community in Tucson, Arizona, you'll find yourself invited to a commencement. Your Commencement Day is the day you sign your residency agreement and pay your entrance fee. Explains Gale Morgan, vice president of sales for Mather LifeWays, "We call it a commencement because it's the beginning of their *repriorment*. Of course, we've renamed *retirement* to be *repriorment*, when one is creating new priorities and new passions in their life."

✓ When you arrive for your Commencement Day, you'll literally walk a red carpet, complete with stanchions and velvet ropes. You'll notice balloons in the room and an air of celebration.

✓ In the meantime, there is much happening behind the scenes that you may not notice. About 10 minutes before you are done, a cart draped with a white cloth is parked just outside the door. It is filled with white dipped chocolate strawberries and champagne, and garnished with a beautiful edible orchid.

✓ A 10-minute warning goes out. It ensures that every Experience Manager and available staff member is waiting to celebrate with you. At the conclusion of the commencement, the doors open and in they come! You'll be applauded, welcomed, and treated to a champagne toast (or sparkling cider, if you prefer), generally celebrated.

✓ A photo is taken; on move-in day, you'll find the framed photo in your apartment with a commemorative cork from the bottle of champagne and other special treats.

✓ Says Gale, "We've also put all the staff on notice. Everyone knows who is expected and who will come with them.

Each person is prepared to call everyone by name, right down to the dog if they have one!"

✓ The Experience Team also works hard to get to know their new residents and do something to personalize each person's special day. For instance, one single woman mentioned that she was most looking forward to not having to cook dinner. "In fact," she said, "I've actually stopped buying cereal because when you live alone, it's too easy to just eat cereal for dinner." On her Commencement Day, she was treated to a mini-variety pack of cereal, because, as they told her, "You can have cereal now! We've got dinner covered." When asked about the response to this process, Gale says, "It's been incredibly positive. This is a very emotional process for people. Once the papers are signed, they are relieved it's behind them and then the party is there. They are surrounded by friendly faces, all making conversation, and providing them with a very warm welcome."

✓ Of course, Gale and the rest of the Experience Team understand how important it is to *know your audience*. There are times when an all-out celebration may not be appropriate. "If we know there's been a recent loss of a spouse or an exceptionally emotional experience, we do dial it back. Sometimes you're hugging and holding their hand more than you're toasting."

Salmeron Financial Prepares to Wow

Rick Salmeron, a financial planner based in Dallas, Texas, does several things to ensure his prospects and clients have an amazing arrival experience. For instance:

✓ When he has the opportunity to meet with a potential client for the first time, Rick sends that client a 10-question online survey. Most of the questions are related to finances, risk tolerance, and other expected details. However, the last question gives him the insight he needs to begin to build a relationship with the client. The final question reads, "Won't you tell us about you? What do you like? Where have you traveled? What's your favorite cuisine? Paint us a picture of you as a person." Rick finds that question #10 is the key to getting to know clients and personalizing their experience. "Some people," he jokes, "really take advantage of it and spill their guts! When they do, I get a head-start on understanding what makes them happy."

✓ Next, in advance of their initial consultation, he'll send an email that reads, "Tell us what your favorite non-alcoholic beverage is for this time of day. We may just have it ready for you!" While not everyone takes advantage of this extra, the ones who do are absolutely delighted. Every possible non-alcoholic drink there is, is on the table. Rick promises, "When people write that they wouldn't mind a tall, nonfat soy latte with stevia, Melissa (his administrative assistant) is off to Starbucks to bring it back for them. If they want a beet, celery, ginger, and apple smoothie, we'll have that for them, too."

✓ When the client arrives, they'll notice a chalkboard with a welcome greeting, personalized with his or her name and decorated with elaborate drawings. These are created by the "Director of First Impressions," otherwise known as Rick's 14-year-old daughter.

✓ If a potential client was a referral from a current customer, Rick sends the current customer handwritten thank-you note. In it he specifically pledges to give the friend, family member, or colleague the same high-level of service and care he or she receives from the team at Salmeron Financial. A special gift card is an added bonus!

You'll learn more about how Rick keeps the red carpet out for his long-time customers in Chapter 4.

The Village Coffee Shop Celebrates Village Virgins

Should you ever find yourself at The Village Coffee Shop in Boulder, Colorado, be prepared for a *very* warm welcome. Guests who are eating at the restaurant for the first time are dubbed "Village Virgins."

✓ If you're found out, an announcement will be made to the whole restaurant: "Attention, everyone! We have one Village Virgin sitting right here." At that point, every employee and guest of the restaurant cheers. "That's how we welcome people to the family. We clap and cheer for them and embarrass them—just a little bit—for a minute," says owner Shanna Henkel. "The tradition pre-dates me and I've been here 19 years. It has a wonderful impact on the new guest who is, more often than not, surprised by the 50 or 60 people clapping for [him or her]."

It's no surprise the Village Coffee Shop has been named the "Best Place to Feel Welcomed to the Family" by a local publication.

The warm welcome must work. The 890-square-foot restaurant space is often packed. "We have people who come back over and over again. I am currently serving people working on their master's thesis, whom I waited [on] when they were toddlers. I'm so proud of them!" Shanna proclaims. "The quality of our customers is not to be denied. People who come to eat in a neighborhood diner when they are surrounded by many fancier options in Boulder, Colorado, are just the coolest people!"

Bellhops Keep the Emergency Room Hopping

If you've ever had to go to the emergency room of a hospital for something that wasn't immediately life threatening, you've probably been frustrated by the long wait and lack of communication. It's a frustration that is shared by many patients, in many hospitals, everywhere.

When Southside Hospital in Bay Shore, New York, part of the Northwell Health System, became a trauma center in 2014, the resulting increase in volume at the emergency room was maddening to patients and staff alike. "We were pretty much busting at the seams in terms of patients," remarks Patricia McColley, the service excellence Manager for the Emergency Medicine and Trauma Department. "I decided something needed to be done for those who were kept waiting, and that's when we came up with the Compassionate Care Model, which uses Bellhops to deliver this comfort care."

Patty, as she prefers to be called, also managed the volunteer department and found she had a great resource in the teenagers and young adults, many of whom are medical students in their high school or college program. Her idea is to train them to be excellent clinicians, but with a hospitality focus, who can become agents of compassionate care.

✓ The Bellhops are a team of volunteers who work four-hour shifts making people comfortable while they wait in the emergency room. They are trained in basic "rounding," offering basic comforts such as pillows, blankets, coffee, or anything special a patient or family member might need while they wait. They check in to see if they've eaten and show them general hospitality. The snazzy blue vests they wear help to identify them. For Patty, this program is a dream come true. "I love watching how they've embraced it with such eagerness. They are such an incredible group of folks who want to make difference. To get them at such an impressionable age when they are just starting their career, it allows us to truly create customer service focused clinicians."

✓ The volunteers themselves have taken the program to a whole other level. The Bellhops are led and trained by Vlady Delos Santos, a patient care liaison, and 17-year-old Kyle Hopps, a senior volunteer. "I call them Batman and Robin. They are just amazing!" exclaims Patty. "They are fantastic in terms of their creativity and they love the fact that I will consider any idea they have that makes a difference to the patient. We discuss cost, logistics, how to make it work. They thrive on that! The whole concept is just delicious to them." At least two of those ideas have been a hit with patients and their family members:

✓ They've created the Coffee Cart, which is a cart that rolls around in the emergency department. Vlady offers customized iced coffee that looks like a mudslide. It's chocolate and just visually beautiful. Their iced tea is garnished with mint and oranges and lemons. It's appealing and takes the patient's mind off his or her fears and stress and the long wait. "They love it," says Patty. "Photos and comments about the cart have been sent out on the Twitter universe a ton of times." Once they are done serving the people waiting in the ER, they'll run past the nurses' station with anything that's left. "The nurses and doctors definitely look forward to the coffee cart!"

✓ One night Vlady and Kyle decided to put together a comfort kit that has now made its way into the Bellhop program. Each kit contains eye masks and earplugs, as the ER is not a quiet place where the lights can be turned on or off. The kit is available in English and Spanish, with a note that encourages the patient to "enjoy and sleep while you're waiting for your room." Vlady won Employee of the Month for her innovative idea and excellent implementation.

The Bellhop Program has made a real difference to the patients and their family members. One person wrote, "My sister was being admitted and leaving her six-year-old and two-year-old for the first time without their mother. This was very distressing to her. Vlady, with her kind spirit, was able to comfort my sister and actually made her laugh. I was impressed with all they do to make patients and their families feel comfortable."

✓ For patients waiting six or more hours, they've created an amenity kit. This includes the earplugs and eye mask, along with sanitizer, shampoo, body wash, a comb, and a toothbrush and toothpaste, as well as a Sudoku book, a pencil, a blanket, and some cozy blue socks. This is delivered to patients along with a sincere apology any time they have to wait on a stretcher for more than six hours. When they make it to a bed, and the nurse sees the blue package, it's a signal that this patient has waited a longer than usual. The nurse can apologize once again for the delay and assure the patient that he or she will be well cared for. It shows the connection between the emergency department and the inpatient location, where patients may remain for the duration of their stay.

Patty also understands how important transparency is to the patient waiting in the emergency room. Currently she's working with the medical team, which now gives her information on how long a patient might have to wait:

✓ "I'll ask at the nursing station: *What challenges do we face today? What do we have going on? How long is the wait?* Once we have that information, the Bellhops can be communicative with the patients and their family members. A four-hour wait is horrific any way you look at it, but at times, it's unavoidable. At least we can explain, and they can make their plans. It's about communicating and then delivering."

Sounds like an extraordinary marriage between healthcare and hospitality.

Every Moment Makes a Difference

I was introduced to Patty by Sven Gierlinger, who is the vice president and chief experience officer of Northwell Health, formerly North Shore LIJ Health System, in New York State. He and I share a common philosophy: One of the core messages I share with my audiences is the idea that every interaction you have with another person (whether customer, employee, friend, or family member) makes a bigger impact than you realize. Every single interaction matters. Every moment makes a difference.

Sven agrees, and his personal story proves the point.

Several years ago, Sven was diagnosed with Guillain-Barre Syndrome, a debilitating disease that affects the nervous system. It often leads to paralysis and in some rare cases can even be terminal. Thankfully he is now fully recovered. However, for more than a year he went through the entire continuum of healthcare. When he was paralyzed from head to toe, he was totally dependent on nurses, doctors, and other clinicians. Prior to his illness, Sven was one of the pre-opening executives for a new Ritz-Carlton in Washington, DC. His experience within the healthcare system drives his newfound passion for improving the experience of patients by combining warmth and hospitality within the field of medicine in his current position.

His healthcare experience, Sven relates, was made up of many moments. There were high moments and there were low moments, and they were always dependent on the last person with whom he interacted. One particular example that made an impact with him was with a specific nurse who was seemingly cold. "She never smiled. She was rather nasty. Quite frankly, I was often afraid of her. I had been in the hospital for two months. In all that time, she never built a relationship with me. One day, I asked if I could have a shave soon. When you're in the hospital those little things mean so much. She promised that she would do it before the end of her shift. Her shift came and went and I thought: *Why am I surprised? She doesn't like me anyway.* Then, 15 minutes past her shift, the unsmiling nurse walked into the room and told me that she'd already clocked out but then remembered she promised to shave me. Then she did."

"Now," Sven says, "I understood that she cared about me as an individual. My view of her changed almost instantly. However, for weeks before that she had failed to build that relationship. I wonder what would have happened if I had gotten discharged the day before. I would have had a very negative impression of her. I would have wondered why she was allowed to act like that and why the leaders of the hospital weren't paying attention. With that one act, she erased what had happened before and I felt better [about] her. It's not like she began to smile; she never smiled," he laughs. "However, in that moment I understood that she cared."

Sven now inspires the team at Northwell by reminding them that, as he puts it, "every moment that we come into contact with our patients and customers matters."

✓ Never lose sight of the impact you make on other people in any given moment. The choice you make to smile (or not), to follow through (or not), to be empathetic (or not) makes a bigger difference than you will ever know. Choose wisely.

It's a Great Day at Talent Plus!

Talent Plus is a leader in talent-based assessments for employee selection and development based on scientific solutions. You'll be reading a lot about them throughout this book, and I can't tell you how much I enjoyed getting to know them through my research process. We share similar philosophies, and I'd be remiss if I didn't mention that Cydney Koukol, chief communication officer, went above and beyond to secure additional interviews for me with people who were more than willing to share their ideas with you here. Count me as the newest member of her fan club.

Here are three simple but effective ways that the team at Talent Plus makes a grand first impression:

✓ Call the offices of Talent Plus, Inc. in Lincoln, Nebraska, and you'll be greeted by a cheery, "It's a great day at Talent Plus!" Based on what Cydney and others shared with me, I imagine this is more than just a unique way to answer the phone—it's their reality.

✓ If you're a client or prospective customer visiting the office for the first time, you'll receive an *actual* red carpet welcome! A literal red carpet is rolled out in their atrium and the entire team lines up on each side and applauds you as you walk into the building.

✓ At the end of the carpet, guests will notice an electronic sign with their name on it, providing an extra, personalized greeting.

Is it any wonder I felt a kinship with the people at Talent Plus?

✓ Whenever we lead customer service training programs
through my company, Red-Carpet Learning Systems, Inc.,
we also roll out a red carpet. Our client's leadership team
is encouraged to stand on either side and cheer employees
on as they walk into the training room. I can tell you from
first-hand experience that the effect is outstanding. People
walk into the room understanding that this will be unlike
any other training program they've attended. They also
feel appreciated by their managers, who took the time to
be there to provide an amazing arrival experience.

✓ The leadership team at EdenHill Communities, a senior living residence based in New Braunfels, Texas, took this experience to a whole other level. Their training theme was "cruise ship–style" service, and the curriculum was based around the phrase "The EdenHill spirit." Jill Wilson, HR director, assisted by Kim Lanza, training coordinator, ordered cruise ship–style uniforms for the entire management team, complete with captain's livery for CEO Larry Dahl. Each manager had a specific phrase of welcome to say to each team member as he or she walked into the initial kickoff rally. Others were assigned roles such as offering attendees sparkling cider or personally escorting them to their seat. The idea was to give staff members an arrival experience that modeled the type of service they were to give their residents and other customers.

A Doggone Enthusiastic Greeting at the Aloft of Asheville

Stay at the Aloft Hotel in Asheville, North Carolina, and you may just find yourself heading home with a little extra something in your luggage: a new dog, courtesy of the hotel's foster dog-adoption program.

✓ The four-legged hotel family member greets guests in the lobby and is cared for by the staff members. The dog wears an "Adopt Me" vest. Guests are encouraged to interact with the animal and even play with the dog in their room. Once the dog is adopted by a guest, the hotel brings in a new foster dog.

Emma Ledbetter, the assistant general manager for Aloft Hotel in Asheville, North Carolina, was sitting next to a board member of Charlie's Angels Animal Rescue at an event when the idea for their dog- adoption program was born. Touched by Charlie's Angels mission of rescuing adoptable dogs from kill shelters just before their time runs out, Emma thought, *I wonder if we could adopt a dog?*

Actually, it was a perfect fit. The Aloft is the kind of hotel that starts dogs' tails wagging! Canine customers are greeted with treats at check-in. The four-legged guests enjoy a dog bed and water dish in the room, and have their own area out by the pool.

The Aloft chain is operated by McKibbon Hotel Management. As an organization, they encourage the leaders of their 80 hotels to make an intentional effort to give back to the community on a quarterly basis. "Quite honestly," says Lauren Bowles, director of communication for McKibbon Hotel Management, Inc., "we had no idea how successful the adoption program would become. We thought we'd be fostering one dog every quarter." Instead, the first dog was adopted within a few days. Since the program's launch in August 2014, 35 dogs have been adopted (as of this writing) at the Aloft Asheville. Dogs are typically adopted within a couple of days or a couple of weeks. The program has doubled Charlie's Angels rescue numbers.

Says Lauren, "We're hoping to find homes for 50 dogs this year."

The foster dog-adoption program has been a media magnet, landing the Aloft Asheville on the *Today* show, in *People* magazine, and in other national and local outlets. The staff at their new hotel in Greenville, South Carolina, and the team at the Aloft Tallahassee are ready to begin a similar program.

✓ What a great way for the Aloft to extend its relationships with its customers. Guests who have adopted dogs send in photos and stay in touch with both the staff at the Aloft and Charlie's Angels Animal Rescue. "We're currently cooking up some way to celebrate dog adoption anniversaries," says Lauren. Personally, I can't think of a better way to be greeted than with the unrivaled zeal and enthusiasm of a playful pup! The Aloft gives their other canine guests a terrific arrival experience, as well.

The Aloft is not the only place in Asheville where dogs get the star treatment.

- ✓ Barkwells, the Dog Lovers' Vacation retreat, offers luxury, fully equipped vacation rental homes designed for people who travel with their dogs. When guests arrive at the cabin, there is a white board complete with a "Welcome to Barkwells" greeting, and personalized with the human guests and their dog's name.
- ✓ If it is a special occasion, such as a birthday (canine or human), anniversary, or honeymoon, that is also noted on the board, and a bottle of bubbly is placed in the in-room fridge. An event-appropriate flag is even flown outside the cabin.
- ✓ For loyalty program guests who are on their third or more visit, they will find a dog-paw printed bag in the cabin with a handwritten note expressing the hotel's appreciation for their patronage, along with cheese, crackers, and wine from local vendors and local dog treats from 3 Dog Bakery, a favorite among Asheville pooches.
- ✓ During their 10th anniversary, Barkwells hosted "Yappy Hour" every Friday evening from 5 to 6 p.m., providing hors d'oeuvres, crackers, and locally made cheese, wine, cheesecake, and dog treats to two- and four-legged guests. It was an immensely popular event, often resulting in guests booking another stay on the spot.

A Front of the House Welcome

Two organizations close to my heart are Asheville Community Theatre and North Carolina Stage Company, right here in my hometown. Both

Susan Harper, the executive director of Asheville Community Theatre, and Charlie Flynn-McIver, cofounder and artistic director of North Carolina Stage Company, understand that the quality of their stage productions is only half of the experience. Patrons' experiences off-stage or "in front of the house" are just as critical to ensuring they enjoy the show. At Asheville Community Theatre:

✓ The staff are trained to welcome anyone who walks into the building, greeting guests with a friendly smile and offering a tour of the theatre.

✓ The box office staff members walk around the counter to greet patrons and deliver their tickets.

✓ They also block off special seating for problems that might arise. This helps when patrons mix up dates or subscribers forget to make reservations. You might expect they are back-row seats; however, Susan assures me they are really terrific seats.

✓ On opening weekend, a host walks through the lobby offering complimentary champagne; on "Sweet Saturday" they give out chocolates; and on Sunday the cast comes out at the end of the show for a "talk-back," answering questions from the audience.

At North Carolina Stage Company:

✓ Staff and board members who are there to do the welcome or "curtain speech" prior to the show, come early to mingle and personally thank each audience member for attending.

✓ When he's available to be at the show, artistic director Charlie Flynn-McIver will take a peek at the guest manifest for the evening to see which donors will be in

attendance. He makes a point to seek them out, thank
them for coming, and wish them well.

✓ Charlie asks that ushers *not* take tickets from patrons,
but rather ask if they can help them find their seats. It
avoids a backlog of patrons waiting to get into the theatre
and fosters a sense of belonging (with no "gate-keeper"
determining whether they're worthy to get in to see the
performance).

Sometimes You Have to Be a Detective

If you want to make a truly magnificent first impression, it's important to sharpen your powers of observation. Consider the conversation Hans Van Der Reijden, managing director of hotel operations and
Educational Initiatives for the Hotel at Auburn University in Auburn,
Alabama, recently had with his housekeeping staff.

Says Hans, "The other day, I was facilitating the lineup [morning
team meetings] for our housekeepers. I love doing this as it gets my day
off to a really good start, and I love hanging with these ladies in the
morning. I asked them this question: 'Imagine you see a family of four
coming up the elevator to a room that is a double with two beds. What
do you think they are going to need?' They responded, 'They will need
extra towels, extra soap, and shampoo.' 'Correct!' I tell them. The next
question is, 'What do you do?' All the hands fly up and they all say that
instead of asking, they would simply be proactive, knock on the door
with the extras, and say, 'I noticed you coming up in the elevator. You
may need more towels, etc. Here you go!' They added, 'We'd also be
sure to use their names and ask if there's anything else that could be
done for them.' 'You are so right,' I told them."

✓ Hans suggests, "If you observe a customer or group
of customers and you know from their behavior or

circumstances what they're going to need, don't wait until they ask you. Surprise them with your initiative."

✓ Hans continues, "It's important to get to know your regular customers, as well. Be sure to learn all you can about them. For instance, in the restaurant, if someone is highly allergic to seafood and pine nuts and basil, and you start telling them that the special for the night is grilled oysters with a pesto sauce on the side, you've just killed them three times. It's important to recognize what they do like, but also understand what they *don't* like."

Other Times, You're the Informant

Ed Eynon is the vice president/chief human resources officer for KSL Resorts. He has held many other impressive titles as well, including senior VP of human resources for the Cheesecake Factory, and, prior to that, senior VP of human resources and international relations for the Salt Lake City Olympic Committee. As we talked, he reminded me of intertwining both the technical aspects of customer service with the hospitality aspects. We'll revisit this idea later on in the book.

He offers these suggestions for ensuring guests feel the warmth of your welcome:

✓ Smile, make eye contact, and warmly greet guests before they greet you.
✓ Use the 10/5 rule. (Within 10 feet of a customer, smile and make eye contact. Within five feet, provide a friendly greeting.)
✓ Open doors for guests.
✓ Learn to read people if they look confused or lost, so you can proactively assist them.

✓ Maintain eye contact while conversing with guests.

✓ If the guest's name is known, use it.

✓ If you don't know the guest's name, learn it and use it thereafter.

✓ Pass the guest's name on discreetly to other associates.

It's this last tidbit that makes all the difference. It's important to remember that in order to make a truly outstanding impression, the red-carpet treatment must come from everyone on your team. So, work as a team to ensure that it happens!

✓ Ed says, "On the technical side of things, we found years ago at the Cheesecake Factory that one of the most damaging things you could do in a restaurant was to have an unclean women's bathroom. That was a deal-breaker. So we made sure that rarely ever happened."

✓ According to Ed, you also want to ensure that your team members have the information they need in order to effectively answer your customers' questions. He elaborates, "When we did our games [the Salt Lake City Olympic Games in 2002] we made sure our staff and volunteers had pocket tools to help them identify anything in all of the venues. They had schedules and directions on their person so that not only could they be warm and friendly and personalize the experience, but [they] could give [guests] the information that they needed. When you can do that, it's totally different than only having people who are warm and smile. That's a good start but it's not a finish!"

What an exceptional way to ensure you weave both the technical aspects in with the hospitality aspects—for a seamless arrival experience.

Enjoy the Wait at Mama D's

Voted one of the top 100 places to eat the United States in 2014 and 2015, it's no surprise that you might find a two-hour wait at Mama D's Italian Kitchen in Newport Beach, California. What might be surprising is that people come for the wait as much as they come for the meal.

Spencer Forgey, manager at Mama D's, knows which side his bread is buttered on. "How we see it," he tells me, "is that somebody is coming to us. We're so honored. There are thousands of restaurants within just a small radius, and they are choosing us. They are essentially saying, 'We want to give you our money.' We believe there is nothing in it for me, when I am in it for me. Service is an honor. So it is our mission to show them an amazing time from the moment they walk through our doors, not just from the moment they are seated at a table."

Here's what your experience might be like if you visited Mama D's on a Saturday night:

- ✓ On a weekend, you'll find that parking is slim because Mama D's is right by the beach. So you might pull up to the back of the restaurant where they offer valet parking. You'll pull up, get out, and literally walk down the red carpet, complete with stanchions and velvet ropes, as you enter Mama D's.
- ✓ They hire plenty of hosts. For a typical restaurant with a maximum occupancy of 86, you might see one or two hosts. Mama D's has anywhere from six to seven hosts working on a given night.
- ✓ One of those hosts is a "list person." This is the person who runs the list, taking down the names of people who come in to dine.
- ✓ As you are greeted, before you're even able to ask how long the wait is, you'll be handed a piece of bread. Spencer

explains, "The reason people come to a restaurant is that they're hungry. They want to satisfy that need. We don't want them to have to wait." So, you'll get their focaccia bread, baked fresh from scratch every day and straight out of the oven. Once you try the bread, they'll put your name on the list and give you the wait time. The host will offer, "Check in with me as often as you like."

✓ You'll then be offered a menu and a seat in one of the comfortable couches in the center of the restaurant or one of the chairs they have lined up outside.

✓ You'll be offered beer, wine, or another beverage by one of the hosts.

✓ Every 10 minutes, a host will arrive to offer you an appetizer served from a silver platter. Mama D's is known for their outstanding meatballs, and you won't have to wait for them. They're offered to you on the house! You might also get a sample of their delicious cheese tortellini.

✓ If you've come when the weather is cold, you'll be offered a blanket.

✓ In the summer, you and your children will be entertained by one of the best street magicians in Orange County.

"At Mama D's," says Spencer proudly, "our meatballs are outstanding and they've won several awards, but the people aren't coming for our meatballs. They are coming for the experience."

Relax and Roll Out the Red Carpet

"At Innovative Spa Management we focus on delivering 5-star service regardless of whether the spa is in a 3-star hotel or 5-diamond hotel," says founding partner Christina Stratton, of Asheville, North Carolina. "For us it's about taking care of the guests from the moment they make the phone call [to] our spa facility, to the moment they're leaving. We do that through 5-star training." For them, first impressions are all about the details. According to Christina:

✓ They use a minimum of six hot heated towels.

✓ They double handshake their guests.

✓ They refer to them as guests, not clients.

✓ They focus their energy on making every single guest feel like this time is *their* time.

✓ They never want guests to feel rushed off the phone. They take their time to discover guests' goals for the visit. Are they celebrating something? Are they looking to relax? Or do they want something more results-oriented like a facial?

✓ They stand on their tiptoes—literally! They train their team to step up a little bit on their tiptoes, because the voice naturally heightens. It works! Their people relax a little because it makes them feel silly, brings out their softer side, and really changes their vocal timbre.

✓ At Spa Theology, their downtown Asheville location, they surprise each guest with a treat in her locker. It's a little box, wrapped in a blue ribbon that contains the most wonderful, amazing, healthy dark chocolate.

A Red-Carpet Takeoff

As a frequent flyer of Delta Airlines, I've noticed recently that they are placing an increased focus on improving customer experience. Here are some things that I've noticed and appreciated:

✓ Gate agents are making a point to smile, call guests by name, and thank people for their business.

✓ Occasionally, a flight attendant will come by and personally say hello to the frequent fliers on board.

✓ On almost every flight, the crew takes the time to thank military personnel onboard.

✓ If there is a delay in travel, I receive a survey asking me what they can do to improve their service.

✓ Recently, I was thankful to be upgraded to business class, a privilege I'm sometimes granted as a full-fledged road warrior. Prior to the flight, the pilot came out of the cockpit and addressed everyone in the first few rows. He welcomed us to his plane, thanked us for our business, and told us a little bit about what to expect during the flight. He pointed out sites we might see out our windows as we took off and thanked us again for flying Delta. As he returned to the cockpit, there was a murmur of appreciation in the business class section. While pilots often thank passengers over the loudspeaker from the cockpit, this was the first time any of us had received such a personal, face-to-face welcome.

✓ On another flight, it got even better. This time, I was in coach. The pilot stood at the front of the plane and addressed everyone on board. He welcomed us warmly and introduced the flight attendants. He asked us to remember that safety was their number-one concern, and to please pay special attention to the safety briefing. He then shared a little bit about the combined experience that he and his copilot had, and assured us that we were in really good hands. Wow—that's a first-class departure, even for those of us in coach!

The Airline That Gives Passengers a Front-Row Seat

One way to treat a customer like royalty is to provide them with exclusive, one-of-a-kind experiences. This is what they do at Hopscotch Air, an air taxi service that offers private aviation within a 300-mile radius of New York City, at affordable prices. Andrew Schmertz, cofounder and CEO of the company, told me, "Your car is our biggest competitor. We are able to take customers to destinations they would normally drive to, and get them home within the same day. Half of our new customers have never flown on a private plane before." Here's why they are in for a treat:

✓ While passengers have the choice to sit quietly in the back if they prefer, they are offered the opportunity to sit up front right next to the pilot. "While all our planes are equipped with XM satellite radio, in six years of business, I have not heard a story where the customer wants to listen to the radio. They'd much rather talk to the pilot." Captain Chris Dupin, a Hopscotch Air pilot, concurs: "On a typical flight, the customer service is delivered through flight attendants. I really enjoy meeting a customer, shaking hands, and taking their bag for them."

✓ The pilots also serve as coordinators of the customer's travel arrangements. "I see myself as more than a pilot," continues Chris. "I see myself as a trip mission coordinator, and I take a lot of pride in having their rental car ready and waiting at the other end. Some of our customers are not used to the concept of having their car waiting for them."

While you may not be able to offer a "sit up with the pilot" experience, you may be able to offer exclusive access to your customers and coordinate details to an unexpected extent so they feel like they are getting that star treatment.

Treat Customers Like STARS

Penn National Gaming is an entertainment company that owns or operates 26 gaming and/or racing facilities in 17 jurisdictions in the

United States. A few years ago, I had the pleasure of working with them to develop their customer-service training curriculum and train their trainers to deliver it throughout their organization. I was tickled pink to find that their red-carpet customer service philosophy was still in place. Says Maggie Deering, the human resources manager for the Hollywood Casino Joliet, "In numerous cases, our guests are walking away without a tangible product after spending their hard-earned money. It's our job to make sure they walk away having had an incredible experience. Every smile, every answer we give, and every interaction makes up that red-carpet experience for our guest." So, at Penn National Gaming they treat their customers like STARS:

- ✓ **S**mile, speak first, and call them by name.
- ✓ **T**ake responsibility from start to finish.
- ✓ **A**nticipate their needs.
- ✓ **R**ecover with style (when necessary).
- ✓ **S**end them home with a smile and invite them back.

Just a quick note: I think one of the best ways to ensure you have a repeat customer is to personally invite him or her back. It helps to add a personal touch. "Come back and see us again! Ask for me. My name is Donna. I will personally ensure the red carpet is rolled out for you."

We Roll Out the Red Carpet, Not the Red Tape

That promise is front and center on the Website for the city of Ball Ground, Georgia. Of course, whenever I see something related to red-carpet customer service, I have to investigate. My research led me to the city manager, Eric Wilmarth. "Well, unfortunately, one of the things government has become especially known for is red tape and bureaucracy," he says. Agreed. "We are the northernmost city in the Atlanta metropolitan region, and so many places have benefitted from great economic growth because of the location to Atlanta and

Hartsville International Airport. [Because] the city...is farthest north, you can get skipped over a lot. So, we needed to do something to set ourselves apart."

So they cut the red tape. It began with a one-day planning session about seven or eight years ago. The mayor at the time was a banker and he was in the process of expanding his business. Shortly after the planning session, he sent Eric an e-mail. It included a three-page list of everything they had to do before they got a permit to build their new bank. The same week, Eric received an e-mail from a council member who was in the sign business. He was told he had to meet with four different committees to put up a simple sign. He wrote, "We never need to get to this point." Message received. The city leaders made a list of the permits that were essential for the safety of the community, and another, presumably longer list of those that were put in place to make money (or, "for lack of a better way of saying it, to tell people *you're not quite smart enough to do this on your own*"). The planning committee asked themselves, *Do you really need a permit from your local government to have your kitchen cabinets refaced?* The answer was a resounding no.

Is it working? "Well," says Eric, "we are attracting small business. We will have five new businesses open within the next month."

That's not all they are attracting. Two years ago, the City of Ball Ground registered with a program called Film Ready Communities. In 2015 they landed their first film and it was a doozy. Tom Cruise was coming to town to shoot a movie titled *Mena*. "Two members of the film crew are actually thinking about moving here. I think it's because of the reception they received and they way they were treated," surmises Eric. "Sometimes people see Hollywood coming and see dollar signs, thinking, *How much can we charge them in permit fees?* They were pleasantly surprised that we didn't charge them for a permit." Instead, they asked the crew to use as many local contractors as they could to turn their town into the setting for *Mena*. They asked that the crews be fed locally, use local business, and work with the businesses to ensure they'd be made whole if they lost money because of the filming process. "I think that's just another thing we do differently here in Ball Ground. When Hollywood comes calling, it's not about charging them a $25,000 permit fee. It's about ensuring our local businesses are impacted in a positive way," says Eric.

Sounds like a lot of red carpet without the red tape!

Be Ready With the Solution

Barry Maher is a professional speaker and the author of several books including *No Lie: Truth Is the Ultimate Sales Tool* (McGraw-Hill). When he arrived in Virginia late Friday night for a Saturday-morning keynote, he discovered his luggage was lost. "Normally," he says, "I travel in clothes that are at least acceptable to do a presentation [in]. In this case, I'd spoken the day before, and it had been a long day. I was a mess and the clothes were a mess. My presentation was at 11 a.m. By 9 a.m., my luggage had still not arrived." Someone recommended Davidsons Clothing for Men in Roanoke. He arrived, however, to find that they didn't open for another hour. This would be too late for his speech. However...

✓ One of the employees of the store saw him walking around out front. Barry explained the situation, and he opened the store early and let him. "They were amazing!" exclaimed Barry. "I don't have your standard off-the-rack body, but they went through their entire store trying to find me something that would fit. We were close, but no cigar. So they made several calls until they found someone willing to hem the suit. The owner was about to drive me clear across Roanoke to get my pants hemmed when they found a place around the corner that was willing to open early." Thanks to the team at Davidsons, and the local alterations place, Barry made it to the stage on time, and both firms earned a raving fan who has told their story to many.

Blessings to Go

✓ As you enter Marywood Health Center in Grand Rapids, Michigan, you're not only greeted with the warm, friendly smile of the front-desk receptionist, but with a big basket full of blessings. Each blessing is typed up on a colorful slip of paper. You are encouraged to take one as you enter or depart. It's a little prayer to carry with you along the way.

A Great Lakes Thank You

✓ Cofounders Spencer Barrett and David Burke have included handwritten thank-you notes in the shipment of every order they send out, ever since their company, Great Lakes Clothing Co., was founded in 2012. "Our brand really hits home with people. Those of us from the north great lakes region for whom spending time with family and friends at the cabin are our favorite childhood memories—that's who our brand is centered [on]. So we want to create that same emotional connection with everything we do," says Spencer. When they know something about the person who submitted the order, they'll add a little comment meaningful to you. I experienced this firsthand when, after I placed my order, I received an amazing shirt and a handwritten note from Spencer referencing our call and the fact that my husband is from Minnesota. "We get random e-mails and voice mails all the time from people thanking us for our thank-you note. We're committed to making the impersonal experience of online shopping personal again."

✓ Seven days after you make a purchase with Great Lakes
Clothing Co., you receive an email thank you and a
request for a review. Every customer who leaves a review
receives 10 percent off his or her next purchase. They've
had an overwhelming response of reviews with an average
5-star rating.

There's a Prize Inside

Susan Walton is the owner of Move Sport, Inc., and the developer of
RecoFit Compression Gear for cyclists, triathletes, and runners. She
was thinking about what she could do to stand out from her bigger
competitors when retailers ordered her products to sell in their stores.
She remembered how much fun it was to open a Cracker Jacks box as a
child. Says Susan, "You know you're getting a prize. Even though you
know it's going to be something small, you can't wait to open it and see
what you get. So, I thought, maybe I could put a prize inside my boxes!"

✓ She partnered with other Boulder, Colorado, businesses
that provide sample-sized products that would appeal to
her market. She includes a flyer that tells the story of the
company, as well. "I want them to be excited to open up
the box and think, *Oh! What did Susan send us this time?*"

She laughs, "One store owner was so excited that he ordered every
company's product because he wanted to be the coolest running store
on the East Coast."

Little Touches That Make You Smile

When I travel to speaking engagements, as you can imagine, I have
stayed in my share of hotels. It's always a treat to stay in a 5-star, luxury hotel or resort. However, I *expect* the five-star service there. It's the

details provided by singular employees in the more economical hotels that really make me happy. For instance:

- ✓ At Stony Creek Hotel and Conference Center, I arrived back in my room to find this note from the housekeeper in response to my tip: "Thank you! Although it may be a gloomy day, don't forget to smile." I smiled then and there.
- ✓ I walked into my room at the Hampton Inn in Birmingham, Alabama, to find a bag of microwave popcorn labeled with this question: "Did we make your stay POP? If not, please see the front desk with your concerns and comments."
- ✓ A colleague and I have stayed at the Hampton Inn at Barnes Crossing in Tupelo, Mississippi, several times. Truth be told, there are other hotels closer to our client's location. However, we return again and again because of the outstanding service given to us by the employees of this particular Hampton Inn. There's nothing flashy about their service experience. There isn't one particular thing that caused us to say *wow*. Rather, it's the consistent execution of the basics that has blown us away time and time again.
- ✓ Regardless of who is at the front desk, we are greeted warmly, by name, with eye contact, smiles.
- ✓ When we commented on missing out on the famous Hampton Inn cookies on our first night there, an employee named Felicia made sure we received plated cookies, fresh from the oven, the next evening.
- ✓ When employee Cynthia noticed me waiting in line behind a family to get my morning coffee at 5 a.m., she whispered the location of another pot so I didn't have to wait.
- ✓ When we needed a place to meet for business, employee John was right on it.

- ✓ Each morning at breakfast, employee Annie was there with a smile and some southern hospitality.
- ✓ Perhaps my one of my favorite moments happened when I arrived for my second stay within a couple of months: The front-desk team remembered me and welcomed me back like an old friend.

The staff members at Hampton Inn at Barnes Crossing are masters of the simple act of paying attention and being there to serve. Best of all, the service is consistent regardless of who is working that day. When it comes to red-carpet customer service, consistency is key. The little things make such a difference when each employee is trained to create a welcoming experience for customers. It often doesn't take much to create a memorable moment that turns a guest into a happy customer.

I received so many great examples of the little-things-that-mean-a-lot concept when I stayed at the Marriott at Legacy Town Center in Plano, Texas. For instance:

- ✓ When I checked in, the front desk agent came out from behind the desk to hand me my keys and personally guide me to the elevator and restaurants. What a lovely, unexpected personal touch.
- ✓ When I told the front desk agent to do whatever was easiest for her, she replied, "We are here to serve *you*, Ma'am."
- ✓ They gave me a choice. When I said, "I'll take Diet Coke or Diet Pepsi—whichever you have," the server replied, "Which would you prefer? The decision is yours." Then he brought me two Diet Cokes!
- ✓ Upon learning that I'd be having breakfast alone, the host of the Copper Bottom Grill at the hotel offered me a newspaper to read while I dined.

Communication Makes Tails Wag

When you leave your precious pets in the hands of someone else, communication is oh-so-important. My husband and I have been "parents" to a beautiful, now-deceased Maltese named Snowball and are currently Mom and Dad to two rescue Shih-tzu mixes named Moxie and Tonks. (My science-guy husband would not like being called Dad, as he says it's biologically absurd. But you and I know the truth.) We have left our dogs and our home in the care of Nancy, with "Your Place and Mine" pet sitting, and Magda, of "Miss Jane's Pet Sitting," both in Asheville, North Carolina.

✓ What we most appreciate about both services, in addition to the wonderful care they take of our little sweethearts, is the constant communication from our pet sitters. In both cases, we receive daily updates via text, complete with pictures and video. In fact, as I write this manuscript, my husband and I are in Washington, DC, for a conference, and just received an update about Moxie and Tonks. Though we're slightly insulted that they don't seem to miss us all that much, we're relieved they are happy and safe, and it helps us enjoy our vacation.

Kanyon's Story

My passion for delivering red-carpet customer service is such that I am excited about all of the "501 ways" detailed in this book. However, some stories touch the heart more than others. Kanyon Hillaire's story is one of those. Kanyon is a technician for Safelite AutoGlass in Portland, Oregon. Each morning, it is his practice to call his customers to go over some details and offer them an estimated time of arrival.

✓ One particular morning, Kanyon reached a customer who he soon learned was deaf. He knew that communicating during a job is crucial. Customers must understand how long the repair or replacement will take, when it's safe to drive the car, and what they can expect during the appointment. Kanyon was quick to think of a solution. He called a friend who knew sign language and asked her to record a message for him. "I could have written everything thing down for my customer," Hillaire explained, "but have you ever seen someone after you speak to them in their native language? If not, try it sometime. Just learn a little bit and that person becomes more relaxed and they feel more comfortable. For me, customer service is more than doing a good job. Customer service is allowing that person to feel comfortable and safe. Then they can trust me when I am working on their vehicle." But the ripple effect of red-carpet service didn't end there.

✓ Safelite's executives were so impressed with Hillaire's innovation that they pledged to develop official company videos for the deaf and hard of hearing for all their technicians to access when needed. Spanish language videos quickly followed. The company will track feedback and need for these videos before determining whether to expand into additional languages.

Safelite AutoGlass has a company commitment to delight customers and create memorable experiences. I'll bet you'll agree that on that day, Kanyon delivered! This story and Kanyon's actions reaffirm my belief that every single interaction makes a difference, and that each person makes a greater impact with his or her day-to-day choices than he or she even realizes.

Want to roll out the red carpet for your customers? Choose, as Kanyon did, to take an ordinary interaction and turn it into an extraordinary encounter. You can learn more about Kanyon's story here: *http://youtu.be/lbsyEMtUGEk.*

Telephone Tips for Making Great First and Last Impressions

When you are talking on the phone, the words you use are only 20 percent of what gets communicated. Eighty percent of your message is communicated through nonverbal cues: body language, facial expressions, and so on. On the phone, obviously, you don't have those means of communicating at your disposal, so your tone of voice, your volume, your pitch (high or low), and your enunciation are critical to telephone success. Here are some of the tips that we teach in our Red Carpet Learning Systems Telephone Training Class for making outstanding first and last impressions:

- ✓ Stay upbeat, warm, and friendly. A higher pitch in your voice communicates joy and happiness. A lower voice communicates empathy and seriousness.
- ✓ Speak loudly enough for the person on the other end of the phone to hear you, but not so loudly that he or she has to hold the receiver 10 feet away from his or her ear.
- ✓ Be sure to speak clearly. If you constantly hear people say, "Could you repeat that?" you may need to practice your diction. Tongue twisters help!
- ✓ Use your company's standard greeting; if there isn't one, create a friendly, upbeat greeting that identifies the company and the department they are calling, gives your name, and offers help. Make it short and sweet!

✓ Take note of your caller's name. Write it down as soon as you hear it. Use it once or twice within the context of the call.

✓ Use words and phrases that instill confidence in your customers. Say goodbye to "Um," "Yeah," "Okay," and "No worries!" Replace them with, "I'd be happy to help!" "Absolutely," "My pleasure," and "I can definitely check on that for you!" Instead of "You need to talk to Sue about that," say, "Sue is the absolute best person to handle that for you. May I put you on hold while I transfer the call to Sue?"

✓ Always ask customers if you may put them on hold. When they agree, say thank you. Check back in every 30 to 45 seconds or so. If it's going to take longer than three minutes to research a question, let the caller know and ask if you can call him or her back within a specific time frame.

✓ End the call by asking, "While I have you on the phone, is there anything else I can help you with?" Of course, help them if they say yes. Then, thank them for calling.

These are just a few terrific tips to improve your telephone interactions. If you have some of your own, I'd love to hear them. Remember: You never have a second chance to make a first impression. Be sure your first impression on the phone is a red-carpet one!

E-Mail Impressions

Rick Conlow and Doug Watsabaugh make some great suggestions for making a great first impression via email in their book *Susperstar Customer Service* (Career Press, 2014). Here's what they say about how to write a dynamic e-mail that differentiates you professionally and positively:

✓ Define a specific subject (e.g., "Warranty Information on XYZ Television" or "Order Follow-Up for Your Purchase on date/time").

✓ Give a greeting.

✓ Outline what you want or need in the body of the e-mail.

✓ Include bullets on key points.

✓ Close with an appropriate salutation.

✓ Add a P.S. to give value.

✓ Include an appropriate attachment.

Quick Tips

✓ Ruby Receptionists—or, as they are affectionately known by their customers, Callruby.com—are a great resource when you don't have the resources to hire a full-time receptionist, but want a friendly, real person is answering your phone during working hours.

✓ One of my clients, Devonshire of PGA National, remembered that their vendors also deserve to receive a little red-carpet treatment. Knowing they spend much of their day on a truck making deliveries, they provide snacks and drinks for each vendor that stops at their property.

✓ Korey Hampton, co-owner of French Broad Adventures Rafting and Ziplines in Asheville, North Carolina, knows that using humor is a great way to make red-carpet first impressions on her guests. The company, which opened in 2002 with three employees, took 750 people on adventures that first year. In 2015, they had 85 employees and welcomed more than 20,000 guests. They have enjoyed double-digit growth every single year due to word-of-mouth advertising. In their business safety is paramount, but it is delivered with a sense of fun. Says Korey, "It's our job to ensure everyone is safe and entertained along the way. The standing joke is, 'We're funny, if you can stand bad jokes!' she laughs. "Whether you go ziplining or rafting, we provide an orientation on everything from the gear to do's and don'ts. It's not just your typical safety speech. We have found that, throughout the years, if you just run through a list of instructions, it gets boring. The problem is, when it's boring, people don't listen. This is important information for them to know." The guides give customers a clipboard and ask them to ensure they don't miss anything. They tell jokes, and make it fun and interactive. People laugh. But, more importantly, they learn at the same time. "For example," says Korey, "we'll often tell the guys that if they fall out of the boat to make sure they hold their feet together...so they aren't romancing any of the stones. It just adds a level of humor to everything we say!"

✓ After they take a phone reservation at French Broad Adventures, the team personalizes the experience by sending an e-mail from the very person who took the phone call. Three days after their trip, clients get a follow-up e-mail from the same person. "We have over 20,000 customers a year, so it's a real *wow* for them to get a personalized e-mail," says Korey.

✓ Anticipating customer needs is a terrific way to make an excellent first impression. When Anne Newsome of HealthySouthernMama.com and her husband traveled to Vietnam to complete their son's adoption, they stayed at the Sofitel Hotel in Hanoi. There they had the greatest customer service experience of their lives. They had just wrapped up their son's adoption process and had flown from Saigon to Hanoi for some final appointments before flying back to the United States. Their son was 14 months old but sick and delayed developmentally due to malnourishment, and was running a fever. As they entered the lobby, the hotel staff offered to take them straight to their room so they could get comfortable right away. They then took care of the check-in with Anne's husband so that she and her son could rest. Says Anne, "We were amazed at their level of attentiveness. It is difficult to find good customer service, and so to have this high level of customer service felt amazing, especially on our first foray into international travel and this new experience of adopting our son."

✓ Diane Anderson, owner of Have a Happy Dog training company, invites her best customers and referrers to a dog and owner pool party once a year.

✓ Communication with your customers is key. Media and public relations professional Kim Parker writes, "Mr. Ford from Bellevue Middle School is the best driver ever. He just sent me a text to let me know that my son has a substitute driver, so we won't be worried if the bus is off schedule."

✓ The Dolce Hotel and Conference Center in Atlanta anticipates guests' needs by placing large bins full of umbrellas at every door. As a guest on a day it was raining, I greatly appreciated this thoughtfulness.

✓ A thrift store in Hendersonville, North Carolina, has a great way of anticipating customer needs. They keep a list of regular customers who like certain items. For instance, if someone always comes in looking for interesting hats, she gets put on the list. When a unique-looking hat arrives, they always call her.

✓ When my husband and I dined at the Barter Theatre Café in Abington, Virginia, we enjoyed the unique way they call customers up to the counter to get their meals. Instead of calling me by my name, they assigned us celebrity names. I was "Jane Fonda," but I overheard other celebrities such as "Judy Garland" and "Tom Cruise" being called to pick up their lunch. What fun!

✓ Ask your customers the right questions. When I left one hotel to go home (my favorite destination), the front desk asked me how my stay had been. I replied, "Fine." Then she asked a question that made me think: "What could we have done to make your experience with us even better?" Now *that's* the real question. If you want to embrace a philosophy of continuous improvement, ask questions of your customers that invite helpful feedback.

Keeping Up With the Times

✓ The Hotel at Auburn University has served as a testing site for UberGuest, a new system using GPS technology to enhance the guest experience. It's the brainchild of Klaus Peters, who has a long history of managing high-end hotels. "I realized there was a missing link to providing a personalized experience," says Klaus. "In order to provide true, automatic personal service, we need to recognize the customers before they arrive." If you download the UberGuest app, you have the ability to fill out your profile with everything from personal preferences to peanut allergies. When you are within 10 miles of the hotel, the staff is alerted and is prepared to greet you by name. In fact, whether you head to the hotel gym, a restaurant on the property, or a retail shop, you are greeted by name. Equipped with the information you have provided, the staff are then able to personalize, surprise, and

delight you as the occasion arises. I asked Klaus what
the response was at the Hotel at Auburn University, and
he said, "People loved it! Those who were uncomfortable
with the idea just didn't download the app. However," he
assured me, "the staff doesn't know where you are, just
how far away you are. Once you're out of a 10-mile range,
the tracking disappears. The system is meant for high-end
hotel guests who want to be recognized by name, greeted
at the door, and leave the long front-desk lines behind."
At the time we spoke, UberGuest was still in the development phase. However, Peters expected to be able to make it
available to high-end hotels soon.

✓ BFAC.com is another company that offers a similar mobile
app to other types of organizations. In fact, the app is
developed specifically for your organization. When your
customers download the app, and are within a specific
range of your company, you can send them a text message encouraging them to visit or thanking them for
their patronage. Brad McMullan, founder of BFAC.com,
is a passionate advocate of using apps to enhance the
customer experience. "I have to go where the consumers
are," explains Brad. "People have their cell phones within
three feet of themselves at all times. Today [according to
his research] there are more than 34 million active cell
phones in the United States. According to the Luxury
Institute, people view a brand or business more favorably
if they have an app than if they don't."

There is no doubt about it: Technology has changed the way people
do business. In order to make great impressions on a new generation of
consumers, we must embrace it.

Athough it may be true that you never have a second chance to make a first impression, the last impression may be the one that determines whether you have a one-time customer or a loyal new member of the family. Don't roll that red carpet out at arrival only to roll it back up at the end of a customer interaction. Here are a few ways some organizations have turned a last impression into a lasting impression.

Pets Are People, Too!

Bryan Clayton, CEO of GreenPal, knows that one of the ways to tap into a customer's soul is through their pets. GreenPal is a new service, which has been described as "UBER for lawn care." You basically hire someone to mow your grass via an app on your smartphone. They currently serve Nashville, Atlanta, Tampa, and St. Petersburg, Florida, and they are growing rapidly. "From day one," says Bryan, "we knew we wanted to treat our customers like gold. We gave very personal attention, which is easy when you have a few dozen or even a hundred using your service." Now they have more than 2,000 users, and although they are still very committed to excellence in service, they knew they had to make that personalized attention scalable. He and his cofounders began to notice that during the intake process, many people were mentioning their pets. "It was very important to people that we and their lawn service professional knew about their pets," he says. That's when the idea hit them! One way to make an emotional connection with their customers is through their pets.

✓ If you're a customer of GreenPal and you have pets, your dog or cat will receive a follow-up thank-you note, addressed to them, with a bone or a bit of catnip as a gift. All in all, with shipping, it costs them $2.00 per customer to pull this off and it's earned them repeat business,

Tweets, Facebook posts, and other types of word-of-mouth and viral marketing.

✓ In addition, anyone who uses the service more than two or three times gets a cool T-shirt that blends the GreenPal logo with the state the customer lives in. People love it, and many waste no time snapping a selfie in their new shirt and putting it on Facebook.

A Picture-Perfect Last Impression

✓ When Mark Savoree owned a Ford Lincoln Mercury auto dealership in Paris, Illinois, one of his saleswomen came up with an idea. She said, "Let's take a picture every time someone buys a car, because that's such a big experience in their life." "Back then, we took Polaroids," recalls Mark, "and we'd write their name and the date they bought the car on the little bottom tag. We'd take two. One would go with them and the other we would stick on a corkboard because we were welcoming them to the family!"

✓ Now, Mark and his wife, also the owner of Savoree Properties, take photos of people with their new apartments or homes, this time with a digital camera. They buy small frames and present them as a welcome gift, and people love it! Of course, they also keep a second one on their welcome-to-the-family board in their office.

Picture Perfect Memories

Sheryl Simon, a luxury residential real estate professional with Benoit Mizner Simon and Co. in Weston, Massachusetts, understands that as much as you love your new home, you will also miss the one you're leaving.

✓ She has professional photos taken of the home they're selling, submits them to Shutterfly, and creates a memory book for them. Rather than present it as a closing gift, she sends it to them three or four weeks after the closing with a thank-you note. The photo books provide memories of the home they treasured for so many years are extremely meaningful for the recipients.

✓ She also sends flowers to her clients on the one-year anniversary of their closing.

✓ Sheryl makes red-carpet *first* impressions on parents by providing gifts for their children. Knowing that children who are moving from out of town will need something to keep themselves busy while their parents attend to the details of the move, she provides organic healthy snacks, juice boxes, and toys. She also provides a list of things to do with children in Boston, as well as information about the area schools.

Take the High Road

Paige Arnof-Fenn the founder and CEO of Mavens and Moguls, a global strategic marketing consulting firm based in Boston, Massachusetts, offers this bit of advice when a client decides to go elsewhere:

✓ "I always take the high road. If they decide to hire another firm, I leave the door open for them to stay in touch. If the other firm has made promises I don't believe they can fulfill, I'll be very honest with them. Then I'll kindly offer to be here if it doesn't work out. It's amazing how many times people have come back to us saying they really appreciated how honest and up-front I was with them. I never lie to win their business. I may not always tell them what they want to hear, but we will always speak the truth. In addition, I train my team members to never burn a bridge. It always pays to take the high road."

According to Paige, even firms that don't hire her company have recommended them to others many times. Some decide to hire others and then hire Mavens and Moguls down the road. Says Paige, "They say that we handled ourselves so professionally that they never forgot us."

Caring Memories to Take With You

Having been present while my own beloved father passed away in a hospice house, I have a deep understanding of the special person it takes to work with those who are dying. It was my privilege many years ago to speak for the leaders of the Hospice of Marshall County in Albertville, Alabama. I asked the CEO, Rhonda Osborne, to share some of the ways they deliver a personalized experience to patients and their family members. Here are two that touched me profoundly:

✓ Upon the death of a hospice patient in their home, it is often difficult for families to view an empty bed once the body has been released to the funeral home. Velma, a home hospice care RN, began a Hospice of Marshall County tradition as a final act of kindness. Prior to leaving a home for that final time, the hospice staff member looks for an item to replace the stark emptiness of the bare bed. Many times laying a single rose or flower from an arrangement in the room, a family photograph that includes the deceased, or a Bible turned to a scripture of comfort softens the first look for the family entering the room.

✓ Rhonda and her team also shared this beautiful example: "Hospice of Marshall County strives to express appreciation to all veterans who we are honored to serve. Each

veteran is presented with a certificate of appreciation
for his or her service, reflective of the branch of service, by their care team. If they are served in Shepard's
Cove [HMC's inpatient facility], a quilt resembling the
American flag is draped over the door of the TV armoire.
When they pass at Shepard's Cove, a final act of appreciation and honor is the Stars and Stripes tribute. After
the family has had time to spend with the deceased loved
one, and the body is about to be brought to the funeral
home, it is draped with the American flag, transferred to
the transport gurney, and brought to a central stopping
area in front of the family. The Stars and Stripes tribute
announcement is made and all available staff members line
the hallways with their hands over their hearts. The flag
is folded, military style, by staff members who have been

taught this technique. The flag is then presented to the family with a sharp salute and final verbal expression of appreciation for their loved one's service." Says Rhonda, "I've not left one tribute without a tear in my eye."

These are, I'm sure, the kind of last impressions that people hold in their hearts for a lifetime.

Some Other Quick Tips

- ✓ Gena Pitts, founder and executive director of the Professional Sports Wives Association, advises, "People love it when you check on them beyond the sale, just to say hello."
- ✓ Dr. Dan Margolin of the New Jersey Foot and Ankle Center provides patients with educational letters and post-cards about common podiatry issues.
- ✓ Fiona Brockhurst, client services manager at T-Galleria in Honolulu, Hawaii, shares, "When you make a member's child happy, you've won [him or her] over. That's why we provide toys or picture books about Hawaii for the kids of our loyalty members when they come to visit."
- ✓ Danielle Clay Elia, the owner of ContractorSelling.com, teaches her clients to do a "Happy Check" after a service call. Says Danielle, "The Happy Check or Happy Call ensures that they have given the highest level of service possible. They call with a series of questions to determine the customer's level of satisfaction. Even the call itself is an example of exceeding the customer's expectations."
- ✓ When Allen Klein, author of several books including *You Can't Ruin My Day*, shopped for a hotel to host a high tea for his 60th birthday party, he was blown away

by the service he received by the Ritz Carlton in San Francisco. The meeting professional became a partner in his planning and offered that he could have an *Alice in Wonderland*–themed party out on their terrace. The staff provided an exceptional experience for Allen and his guests from start to finish. Once the party was over, the meeting professional came over and said, "You probably didn't get a lot to eat because you were so busy having a great time. We put together a shopping bag full of food that was at the party so you can eat it at home." This is a perfect example of the Ritz-Carlton's standard to *fulfill the expressed and unexpressed wishes of our guests.*

As you can see, it often only takes a thoughtful gesture to have them at hello and keep them at good-bye. If you really want to create a consistently extraordinary experience, you have to make sure that you are red-carpet ready!

Questions for Discussion

- What opportunities do we have to make a better first impression?
- How could we make a better last impression?
- How do we ensure we're making every moment matter?
- What technology would help us make a great first impression?
- What ideas do we want to try first?

CHAPTER THREE

Get Red-Carpet Ready!

Every single person makes a difference, and every interaction matters. This is precisely the reason I wrote this book. I wanted to give you tangible, actionable ways that you—no matter who you are or what you do for a living—can make a difference through customer service. I want you to experience the *thrill* of the red carpet: where your customer matters, your work matters, and *you* matter. Even if no one else around you gets it, you can make someone's day, and that makes a difference.

At the same time, if you are a leader in an organization and you want to revolutionize and reenergize your culture and customer experience, then you've got to get red-carpet ready! The truth is, your customer service as a whole is only as good as your least engaged employee. Each person your customers interact with daily affects their perception about your company. (Remember Sven Gierlinger's story from the previous chapter?) If you want to be known for a consistently exceptional experience, there's work to do.

According to Nido Qubein, president of High Point University, there are four areas of focus for organizational leaders who want to create an extraordinary experience for those they serve:

1. You must define who you are in such a way that there is nothing nebulous about it. Says Dr. Qubein, "We asked ourselves: *If there are a million people who do exactly what we do, why would someone want to do business with us?* At HPU, every student receives an extraordinary education in an inspiring environment with caring people. We are planting seeds of greatness in the minds and hearts of our students."

2. Next, you must create the system that becomes the foundation of the experience you choose to deliver.

3. Third, you must ask yourself: *How do we create an experience that is congruent with who you are and who you want to be in the future?* "At High Point University," explains Nido, "everything we do is connected to a learning moment that takes you down the path to greatness without your even realizing it."

4. Finally, you must continually interpret what you do for the people you serve and, especially, the people who work for you.

He's right, of course. Whether you are a small business owner, the leader of a mid-sized company, or the CEO of a large corporation, you must string together all your ideas for improving the service experience in a way that is consistent with your and your company's brand. If you have one or more employees, you must have a strategy and a system for:

-   Hiring the right people;
-   Educating them well on your culture and standards;
-   Giving them the appropriate amount of responsibility;
-   Continually communicating your cultural expectations in a variety of ways;
-   Celebrating successes, large and small;
-   And (as Dr. Qubein would say) inspecting what you expect.

Hence, this chapter on getting red-carpet ready! Although it's true that some of the following ideas may not be as easy to implement as others in this book, they are a necessary part of your strategy if want to gain a reputation for consistently delivering red-carpet customer service.

Change Your Paradigm

When I called Spencer Forgey, general manager of Mama D's Italian Kitchen in Newport Beach, California, I was expecting to walk away from the interview with a couple of great examples for the previous chapter. In the end, I got that and so much more! Lucky for Spencer, I had another call scheduled after ours or I might never have let him off the phone. I sat there, absolutely enthralled, as this young manager detailed everything that goes into creating the extraordinary experience customer's have when they eat at Mama D's.

✓ "Let me start by saying that we operate on a completely
   different paradigm than a normal business today," says
   Spencer. "*Paradigm* is a word we use a lot. A paradigm is
   just a fixed way of being. It's how you see the world, often
   looking at it with blinders on. In today's world, there is
   a typical hierarchy in business. The owner is at the top,
   followed by the manager, then the team, and then the
   customer is at the bottom. We have flipped that pyramid
   at Mama D's. For us, the customer is at the top, then the
   servers, followed by management, with the owners at the
   bottom. We don't call them customers. We call them our
   guests and our bosses. In fact, our paychecks don't even
   say 'signed by Keith Davidson, Owner'; it says it's from
   your guest. In our opinion, when you change the way you
   see the world, your world changes. When your guest is

your boss, the experience you want to provide is completely different."

✓ To that end, they pay attention to what the "boss" is telling them. "The first two things I do when I wake up every morning are check the Yelp reviews and the bank accounts," Spencer relates. "Then I text the owner with the information. That's how we start off every day. A lot of people don't like Yelp because they feel it's a double-edged sword. It allows everyone in the world to become a food critic. I, on the other hand, thrive on the feedback. Any feedback—whether it's good or bad—is the breakfast of champions. If someone tells us something wasn't outstanding, now we know and now we can do better."

✓ Speaking of feedback, they ask better questions: "If we ask 'How is everything tasting?' it's easy to get a [noncommittal] response such as 'Good' or 'Okay.' We want better metrics than that. So we ask 'Is everything outstanding?' or 'Has everything been awesome today?'"

✓ At Mama D's, they make a practice of hiring for heart. Says Spencer, "If you're someone who has never worked in a restaurant before, but you have tremendous heart, you'll be much more on the side of the guests and honor them the way we expect." To ensure they find the people they need, rather than wait until they have a position open, they hold regular open interviews. You never know when that perfect team member is going to walk through the door. You don't want to miss out on him or her because you're not currently hiring.

✓ Because authenticity and creative energy are keys to working at Mama D's, Spencer doesn't rely on typical interview questions. He'll try to catch them off guard and ask a question such as 'If you could be any type of animal, what

72

one would you be?' It's the kind of question that reveals personality and allows applicants to show off their creativity. "Most people," says Spencer, "will say 'a cat' or 'a dog.' Then I had a young woman who came in and said, 'That's a really good question. I would want to be an octopus. Wait! No! I changed my mind. I want to be a sloth! They are just so cool.' I thought to myself, *Whoa! She's like us. She's out there and not afraid to show her individuality.*" He hired her, and she turned out to be one of their top employees, working at Mama D's for two years.

✓ On the first day on the job, Mama D's team members go through an orientation program. They leave with a binder and behind-the-scenes information about the business: where they came from, where they are, and where they're going; and their core philosophies. "We break it all down for them and then test them on it," says Spencer. It's also filled with inspirational quotes from people like Gandhi, John Wooden, Vince Lombardi, and others.

✓ Every team member signs a three-page document, agreeing to no complaining whatsoever. "When I first began working at Mama D's," confesses Spencer, "I thought to myself, *How is that possible? I complain all the time. I complain about the traffic—when it's too hot, when it's too cold.* What I began to see is that you just exhaust so much energy complaining and work yourself up for no reason. We create a 100-percent-positive environment because there is no gossip allowed and no complaining. They say that life is 10 percent what happens [to you] and 90 percent how you react to it. We come from a place of *What happens, happens.* Our reaction is what's going to save it."

✓ They invest a lot of money on training. As Spencer says, "We're playing the game at a level that requires it." It must be working for them! While they've spent money on training, they haven't spent one dollar on advertising since their Newport Beach location opened. The long lines out the door all come from word-of-mouth.

✓ "We compare ourselves to a sports team because we're always trying to get better. In fact, we have a team name. It's *The Crazy Ones*. We took it directly from Steve Jobs who said that—I'm paraphrasing—the crazy ones are the people who aren't fond of rules and the status quo. They are the people who will change the world because they don't limit themselves. So," Spencer says proudly, "that's our team name."

✓ As the general manager, Spencer knows he has to model the Mama D's philosophy and mission every single day. "I can't just say 'honor the guest' and not do it myself. I have to do it to the best of my ability and, by doing so, it trickles down through everybody else."

✓ They stay open to new ideas. "I tell all our new hires that we're always looking for ways to get better and enhance the guest experience. If you have any idea you think will help us get better over time, please let us know."

✓ At the same time, Spencer encourages his team to be extremely open to coaching. "We say there are no mistakes, only lessons. So there's no right or wrong. There's just what works and what doesn't work. I tell my new hires, 'You may not understand everything we teach you in the beginning, but when a situation comes up, you'll understand it later.' It's like Mr. Miyagi, from the movie *The Karate Kid*. Daniel couldn't fathom the purpose behind *wax on, wax off* until he got to the tournament and he had that motion down solid. It's important for all of us to stay open to coaching from each other."

74

Clearly, the red-carpet guest experience at Mama D's begins well before the complimentary bread and meatballs come out. They are clear on their mission; they stay focused on their goals; they hire the right people; they orient new hires to their culture and train them; they model their expectations; and they coach and inspire all their employees.

What follows are specific steps you can take to turn *your* workforce into raving fans of your organization who are thrilled to roll out the red carpet for your customers every single day. You'll learn from educational institutions, hotels, call centers, healthcare organizations, and small businesses. First, though, let me share two more tidbits from Mama D's.

✓ Just as Steve Jobs knew, people who are dedicated to providing unique and powerful service experiences know that sometimes you have to break the rules. I was deeply touched by this story that Spencer shared with me: "I've worked in other restaurants in the past. Often, you'd see homeless people come by looking for food. I had a manger who told me, 'Just tell them to go or we're going to call the police' or 'Get them out of here! It's bad for our image.' Then I started working for Mama D's as a server. Addie was my boss at the time, and my predecessor as general manager. At Mama D's we believe that everyone here is up to something great, and Addie embodies this idea. One day, I saw a homeless person walk in to the restaurant during the lunch shift. My immediate reaction was that it was bad for business. It hurt me inside to turn people away like that, but it's what I was taught."

Then Spencer saw something that shifted his paradigm. "Addie noticed the woman bent over the counter counting a few coins.

Quietly, she told the woman, 'Put your quarters back in your pocket and wait right here.' Then she walked over to the chef and said, 'I need a spaghetti and meatballs 911,' which meant this dish is first priority. When we use the code 911, it means a meal must be made right there. No questions asked. Everyone in our restaurant understands this. Within a couple of minutes, the meal came up. Addie put it in a bag with utensils, bread, and cookies, handed it to the woman and said, 'This one's on us!'"

That was the exact moment, according to Spencer, when he truly understood what they're doing at Mama D's and why they're doing it. "I think about that all the time, and, yes, I've even shed a tear or two. What's amazing is that I have the option to do good when the opportunity presents itself and the owner still knows that I've got his back."

✓ A commitment to continuous improvement is shared by many, if not all, leaders of organizations that truly excel in creating a consistently extraordinary experience for their employees and their customers. "The minute you think you've got it all, you've lost it," advises Spencer. "We compare ourselves a lot to a sports team. No football team has ever won the Super Bowl and thought, *Oh, well. We won. We don't have to try as hard next year.* We use the acronym CANI, which stands for Constant and Never Ending Improvement.

This same idea came up in the interviews I conducted with many leaders who are rocking the red carpet customer experience. Kendra Neal, director of client happiness for Ruby Receptionists, a virtual receptionist company based in Portland, Oregon, told me, "We compare ourselves to ourselves. We call it the Ruby Bubble. We never accept that we've done the best we can do because there is always better." Roger Clodfelter, the senior vice president of communications for High Point University, agrees: "We are very hard on ourselves and we never give ourselves an A. Some [leaders] begin to believe their own PR and think their work is the best. I've never met a superior performer that thinks that way."

Are you sensing a theme? One way to ensure you are providing a red-carpet experience for your customers is to work continuously toward improvement, regardless of your remarkable results. As Roger told me when I was writing *The Celebrity Experience,* "Every morning I come in to work and think, *How can we top ourselves today?*"

Hire for Talents

Another commonality among leaders who've become known for their consistently superb customer service is their absolute insistence on hiring people who are the right fit for their culture and who have the natural ability to live up to their expectations. You might say they look for people who bring to the table the specific gifts needed to be able to fulfill their mission, vision, and brand promise. They understand and stay true to the declaration made famous by Jim Collins in his pivotal book, *Good to Great,* that you need "the right people on the bus."

Talent Plus, Inc., a consulting firm based in Lincoln, Nebraska, helps people do just that. Specifically, they help leaders identify people who have the natural talents needed to be successful in their position and their company. According to the company's Website, "Our validated, structured interviews provide a scientific methodology to improve an organization's culture one employee at a time."

The leaders at Talent Plus practice what they preach. Based on my research—including interviews with three of their leaders—they have an amazing culture of their own. They are, incidentally, the ones who literally roll out the red carpet for clients and guests who visit their office. I asked Cydney Koukol, chief communication officer, to give me three practical steps you could take if you wanted to ensure you were hiring the right people for your organization. Here's what she said:

✓ "The first thing I'd say is to make sure that everyone at the senior leadership level believes in the mission. Things work better when they come from the top rather than starting from the bottom and working in the other direction. Having a clear vision that every senior leader is 100-percent behind is imperative."

✓ Cydney suggests that you study your best people. Once you've created a clear vision for the culture you'd like to have, ask yourself: *Are there people working in our company who are already living that way?* Says Cydney, "Whenever we at Talent Plus are going to work with a client, we benchmark their best. Our assessments are always role- and industry-specific. So we ask, 'Who are your best nurses? Who are the best store managers? Branch managers in a bank? Front line employees?' Whatever industry it is, we look at who you tell us your best is and then measure them against who we think are the best. That doesn't mean we're going to tell you your best isn't the best. We just want to understand your culture. When you study your best, you know what you're aiming for."

✓ Have a consistent methodology for selecting people. "Of course," says Cydney, "I believe we do this better than all of our competitors because we study people who do things at a top performance level. The clients we work with want rock stars and people who are at the top of their game. Regardless of whether you use Talent Plus or someone else, it's important to have a consistent process. If you say you are setting out an initiative to change the customer service expression of the company, then you have to make sure that you're doing that in a consistent way. *Every time you select someone, your culture gets better or worse.*"

What this means, of course, is that you must stop hiring every warm body that walks in the door because you need someone now. If you want to create a consistently positive experience for your customers, then you must hold out for customer service rock stars, or for enthusiasm and positivity, or for whatever your culture needs in a consistent way every day. You must do this every single time. Cydney is absolutely right when she says, "What happens when you hire amazing people is that they are disappointed when they have to work with mediocre people. Let's say I work in a call center. I don't want to sit next to someone who is taking terrible care of customers. In reality, I'm in the branding and marketing business and here's the truth: No amount of money you spend will ever overcome a terrible experience your customer has had. It just won't. So, it's critical that every person you hire who touches your customers in some way has the ability to deliver that red carpet service."

Talent Plus uses their own scientific method to hire their own people, as well. Talent Plus was founded in 1989 by Doug Rath, Kimberly Rath, Sandy Maxwell, and Dr. William E. Hall, and was based on Hall's study of positive psychology and human potential. The consulting firm, which was run out of the Raths' back patio in the early years, has grown to an organization of more than 130 associates working primarily in their Lincoln, Nebraska headquarters and their global office in Singapore. Once they have the right people in place, Talent Plus leaders understand the importance of keeping those people focused on the company's culture, values, and goals.

✓ Once a day employees gather for "Formation," a brief company meeting in which they get ready for the day ahead and talk about one of the company's core values. "We took the word *formation* from what geese do," explains Cydney. "When geese fly in formation, they fly in a V. If one [bird moves] out of the V, every other goose cares for...and uplifts [that bird] until [it is] back in the formation. It's

79

about creating a caring workplace where we are intentional about lifting each other up along the way."

✓ A different person leads Formation each day. A monthly calendar lists the topics for each meeting. Employees step up to say they are interested in leading the meeting, and they know, a month in advance, what day is theirs to lead and the topic for that day. We have 30 core values. We call it the Talent Plus Way. Someone reads the value out loud. The person who is leading the meeting has thought about the topic, shares commentary about it, then opens the floor up to related comments. "It's a very short discussion," says Cydney, "but it keeps people focused on who we are and who we want to be as a company. This is how people learn what our policies are, by listening to these topics. This has become our employee handbook. We don't have a binder that people get on day one that says, 'Wear this. Don't wear that. Do this. Don't do that.' It's all about the Talent Plus Way. The value is that if you really have a question above and beyond this, you need to see your leader and funnel it up."

✓ It's important to remember that sometimes you've hired the right person, but you just have him or her in the wrong position. Says Kimberly Rath, Chairman and cofounder of Talent Plus, "We believe everybody has talent to do something well. We had a healthcare client who called to tell us that our science wasn't working. We had interviewed and hired a nurse for them. They put her in the emergency room and she was not doing a good job. We pulled up her talent profile and saw that while she was really great in relational capital, she scored very low in resourcefulness—a critical skill in the emergency room. They recast her in a role in acute care. Twelve months later, she was recognized as employee of the year."

✓ At Talent Plus, they also have what they call the Leadership Lattice. "In today's world," says Rath, "people want a career path. Millennials want flatter organizations without layers of managers. So we created our Leadership Lattice. Everybody in our company can become a director. It may take six to eight years. But there is a path if someone aspires to that kind of title and responsibility."

———

Next we're going to learn about a performing arts center that has figured out a way to ensure that if they hire the wrong person, they don't last for long.

Ask Them to Reapply

Remember how amazed I was by my experience at the Durham Performing Arts Center? Well, it turns out there's a secret to their success and it all begins with—you guessed it—the people they hire. In fact:

✓ Bob Klaus, general manager of Durham Performing Arts Center, told me that the front line staff members have to reapply for their jobs every single year. More than 20 percent don't make it back the following year. That's how committed he is to having the right people in the right positions. Whenever I give that example to my audiences, there's typically a gasp, a giggle, and then a murmur from the crowd. I'll usually follow it up by saying, "While that practice may not be practical in your situation, it's worth asking yourselves this question: *If every employee at your company or in your department had to reapply for his or her job annually, how many of you would you be rehiring?*" At that point, there's a lot of head shaking and knowing looks circulating around the room. Worth thinking about.

✓ When it comes to hiring new employees, Michael Colvin, director of event services, says "I have interviewed 100 people sometimes to hire about 30. It's a long process and tiring and time consuming. However, that's the key to providing this level of customer service. Hire the right people and train them." DPAC provides employees with one day of training. "After that, new hires are positioned with experienced staff for the first few shifts until they get the gist of how we deliver customer service."

✓ Michael is a big believer in the idea that you can't just set people loose and hide in your office. "I walk the floor, and our people know I'm going to be out there. I know they're doing a great job, but it's important to inspect what you expect."

✓ Another secret to DPAC's success is that they use customer feedback to make most of their decisions. Bob and the other managers pore over every comment card and use them to improve the guest experience. One of the moments that blew me away was, quite frankly, when I was in the women's restroom during intermission. The line was long but moved incredibly fast, thanks to an attendant who was personally passing out towels to each person. I mentioned this to Bob, and he said, "When our guests fill out the comment cards or online surveys, they let us know what's important to them. We use that information to continually adjust until we get it right."

✓ Michael suggests that you don't overcomplicate things. "At the end of the day, it's about being nice and sincere to people. It's not about scripting. I'm not going to tell you if every single guest walks past you on the way out, you should say goodnight. We have 2,700 people leaving at once. If you try to say goodnight to all of them, you'll sound phony at best. I hire people who can think on their feet, make positive comments to every third or fourth person, and be authentic in their farewells. All you really have to do is be nice to people. Treat them the way you want to be treated. They'll end up feeling like friends."

Visualize Your Ideal Employee

My friend and colleague Joan Brannick, PhD, is the founder of Brannick HR Connections and the author of *Finding and Keeping Great Employees*, a *Fortune* Best Business Book. She focuses on helping organizational leaders connect the right people with the right strategies to create great relationships, because great relationships produce great results. Joan shares these three tips to ensure you're hiring people that are a fit for your culture and your service standards:

✓ Know what red-carpet customer service looks like and feels like. Gather information from managers and incumbents on the job and from customers to define the skills, abilities, and personal qualities that someone needs to have to provide red-carpet customer service in your company. Then create an ideal candidate profile using this information. You can't be sure you'll find the person you're looking for until you know exactly who you're looking for. Once you've defined your service expectations and your ideal candidate, share this information with everyone who has responsibility in the hiring process.

✓ Examine your hiring process and make sure it aligns with an applicant's ability to provide red-carpet customer service. In other words, your process for hiring people must

be in alignment with your cultural values, mores, and
expectations.

✓ Remember that it's usually easier to train technical
knowledge and skills, and much harder to train for attitude or personality. Given a choice between an applicant
with technical knowledge and skills about the job and/or
industry, and someone with no such knowledge but who is
friendly, a good listener, and interested in helping others,
going with candidate number two is likely a better fit in
terms of delivering red-carpet customer service.

Invite Your Staff to Culture Class

If you're like most of us, you've been through your share of employee
orientation programs. In many cases, you probably sat in the same
room all day long, filling out paperwork, watching boring compli-
ance videos, and listening to someone drone on and on about policies and procedures. You may have left with a head crammed so
full of information you couldn't remember any of it. Or perhaps you
didn't even get an orientation. Instead you were just thrown into
the mix immediately with little training and little direction, and
expected to perform.

Virtually every organization has its "must-haves" for bringing a
new team member on board. What red-carpet service companies know,
however, is that the ingredient most overlooked is introducing a new
rock star to the company culture. That's why new staff members and
faculty coming to work at High Point University attend culture class.

✓ High Point University culture class is half a day long. It
is usually led by Roger Clodfelter, senior VP of communications, with a few appearances by other key personnel,
including Lyndsey Derrow, chief concierge, who addresses

student and customer-service expectations. The class is mandatory for all new hires, and is meant to introduce them to the culture of the university and give them an excellent basis for a successful tenure. Occasionally, others will repeat the class as needed. Roger was kind enough to take me step by step through the class curriculum:

☐ He begins by showing the admissions video. "It's important," advises Roger, "for our staff and faculty to understand how we talk about High Point University to our prospective students and their families."

☐ This is followed by a message from the president, Dr. Nido Qubein. Dr. Qubein, whose personal story is an inspiration to many, is committed to being present and accessible to the students, staff, and faculty of High Point University. As you may remember if you read *The Celebrity Experience*, Nido came to the United States from Lebanon with limited knowledge of English and $50 in his pocket. Through his many entrepreneurial pursuits, Nido was able to graduate from HPU and the University of North Carolina at Greensboro, and become extremely successful, serving on many boards, including BB&T, La-Z-Boy Corporation, and Dots LLC. He is currently the chairman of the board for Great Harvest Bread Company, and the driving force behind HPU's exponential growth over the last few years.

☐ Culture class attendees also learn about the history of High Point University. Roger elaborates, "We show them who we were, who we've become, and the journey we took to get here."

☐ Everyone is given a tour of the university and a photo is taken of the entire group.

85

☐ High Point University's top academic programs are then reviewed, giving each new staff member a broader view beyond his or her own center of focus.

☐ Rogers then spends some time highlighting what HPU gives back to the outside community, instilling a sense of pride in new team members.

☐ He educates the attendees on the economic impact the growth of HPU has had on the community, which is more than $465 million dollars annually. High Point University has won many awards and been the recipient of many honors. These accolades are also shared in culture class. Are you getting the sense that new hires get a real insider's view of the organization that just brought them on board?

☐ "We go through the High Point University Promise," says Roger. The Promise states, in part, that "every student receives an extraordinary education in an inspiring environment with caring people." He talks about the fact that everything they do at HPU is tied to that promise, and to their goal of "preparing students for the world as it's going to be." According to Roger, it's important to arm your staff with the way to talk about your organization. I agree. Your team members can be your greatest advocates if you treat them well and arm them with the information they need to share your story.

☐ During lunch, Lyndsey Derrow takes over, discussing how they deliver that promise every day at HPU. "I ask them for examples of what they feel is good customer service. Then, I share examples from our own university staff. For instance, we have a security guard who everyone knows because she has a huge smile on her face when you come through the welcome center. Her job is campus security. But what she also does is build relationships with students throughout their college career. This is the kind of employee we want at High Point University." Then Lyndsey shares specific steps staff and faculty members can take to deliver an HPU-level of service.

☐ "I talk about how they can take advantage of the opportunities given to them to really succeed here.... We have so many innovators and leaders who come to speak on our campus. In fact, Tom Brokaw was here recently, and Colin Powell. You don't get that kind of opportunity everywhere. I invite our new staff members to jump at the chance to benefit from their wisdom."

☐ Lyndsey tells the new hires about some of the traditions they will be a part of at HPU. "For instance, on Fridays we wear purple," she relates. (It's their way of keeping the Panther spirit alive both on and off campus.)

☐ They inject a bit of fun with "before" and "after" photos related to uniform and dress. "It's important to be conscious of how we're presenting ourselves every day," she points out.

☐ They share more examples of the process behind the promise. "For instance," reveals Roger, "we have a care alert team. They are made up of our student life department, academics, and security. If we see that a student may be having a problem, we're anticipating ways to provide [that student] with assistance. In addition, every freshman has a success coach to help him do well in his first year at the university. Each person who works at High Point University must be dedicated to show that they care. There is no DMV experience allowed at HPU," declares Roger. "We are committed to caring. At the same time, caring does not equal a compromise of our principles and values. This is an academic institution."

☐ "I end with my own version of the Stop, Start, Continue exercise," discloses Lyndsey. "I ask them to share a service strength they would like to continue, a behavior they will stop engaging in, and a service behavior they'll start engaging in from this point forward."

☐ Roger spends some additional time talking about the process behind the promise, learning the importance of removing friction points, walking in the shoes of the students, and "choosing the customer over their own convenience" (a quote, I'm proud to say, he borrowed from my previous book, *The Celebrity Experience*).

☐ Finally they discuss the return on investment for everything they're doing at HPU. The financial returns are, quite frankly, mind-blowing. Their undergraduate enrollment has grown 197 percent in the last 10 years, they've added 970 new positions to faculty and staff, and their operating budget has grown 379 percent. However, there's a more intangible ROI that is perhaps even more important. One enrolled student stated in a letter that after visiting HPU and seeing the "Choose to be extraordinary" messages throughout the campus, all she could think about was how she wanted to be an extraordinary person. She pictured that sign in her head every day. She said no one had ever told her to be extraordinary, and that really resonated with her. That's when she knew she wanted to enroll at HPU.

I'm always amazed whenever I get the chance to visit my friends at High Point University. This time, I was especially touched by the kindness Roger and Lyndsey showed in sharing their culture class secrets. Of course, I shouldn't be surprised; after all, generosity is one of the university's values. As you can see, nothing about this half-day event has to do with signing paperwork, vacation policies, or emergency procedures. This is about immersing people in the values and the philosophy that make up HPU. What would your culture class look like?

Here are some other words of wisdom shared by my friends at HPU related to ensuring you are red-carpet ready:

- ✓ Connect everything you do to your mission and purpose. "Yes," says Dr. Qubein, "we have done a great job stringing a lot of extraordinary moments and experiences together. However, not a single one of them is frivolous. They are all tied to our mission to 'deliver educational experiences that enlighten, challenge, and prepare students to lead lives of significance in complex global communities.'"

- ✓ Lyndsey astutely advises staff to "get out of your bubble." She elaborates, "The fortunate thing for me, being chief concierge, is that I am constantly working with people in other departments. I get to see how other departments work and how other people think. I encourage my staff and others to reach out to someone they may not know. Have lunch outside of your own department, or partner with someone on a project. In the long run, getting out of your own bubble makes you a more successful staff member and ambassador to the whole university or your own company. It's important to know the big picture. It makes you well prepared to answer questions and assist your customers to the best of your ability."

- ✓ Communicate constantly and consistently. "I used to make the assumption," confesses Roger Clodfelter, "that because something was on our Website or in the newspaper, our people knew about it. That's not necessarily true. So now we tell them, and often. We tell them the *what* and we tell them the *why*. You've got to interpret everything you do so your team is on the same page."

✓ To that end, Dr. Qubein leads monthly, mandatory staff meetings. During these meetings, he strives to do three things:

1. Inform: He lets people know what's going on with the university.

2. Inspire: He reads letters of appreciation and acknowledges attendees for their wonderful work. In fact, anyone in the meeting can stand and share a motivating story or words of thanks and praise.

3. Involve: Others also take the stage and share their plans and their successes with the larger group.

Nido also shared a few other golden nuggets. For instance:

✓ "How do you create elegance in the minds of minimum wage workers?" he asks. "Supervision. Make sure the boss knows how to do it and that he or she is watching for you. You must be incisive in the way you evaluate and have multiple points of inspection."

✓ One such inspection they used to practice was to give each vice president, for one week's time, the responsibility for intentionally observing what was happening on campus. At the end of the week, that VP would turn in a report that detailed what was in alignment with their mission, vision, and values, and what wasn't. "What happened," says Nido, "was that, through practice, they became as sensitized to detractors as I am." This is a routine they may be bringing back to life. At the same time...

✓ "Sometimes you have to let go of things," says Dr. Qubein. "Just because we created these ideas doesn't mean they're the best. We try not to keep accumulating without letting something go." This brings us back to Roger's previous point about never giving themselves an A.

As I mentioned in the introductory chapter, readers of *The Celebrity Experience* specifically latched on to the High Point University welcome signs. Hopefully you can see that every little moment like that is connected to a greater purpose. It takes a strategic effort to ensure that each member of your team is delivering an extraordinary experience to your customers.

Here are some examples of how other companies are ensuring that they and their employees are red-carpet ready.

Manifesto of Client Happiness

"This is my passion," says the effusive Kendra Neal, director of client happiness for Ruby Receptionists. Kendra has 28 people on her team who directly or indirectly report to her. "My joy in life is knowing that I am providing them with meaningful, well-paying, fun work to do every day." She and her team clearly have fun at their jobs. At the same time, they are serious about making their clients happy. Kendra understands it can happen only with a strong foundation.

Named one of Oregon's fastest-growing companies for eight consecutive years by the *Portland Business Journal*, Ruby Receptionists credits much of that growth to happy customers. (I, incidentally, am one of them.) According to Kendra, the company grows at a rate of 30 to 40 percent a year. Knowing this, she understands that the systems and solutions created and used by her team must be constantly evolving. She takes several steps to ensure her team is red-carpet ready to deliver client happiness as Ruby Receptionists continues to expand:

✓ **They have off-site meetings.** "We do it in April and September," explains Kendra. "The April meeting is when we fix any system that might have broken during quarter one. During the September meeting, we're heading into the holidays, thinking about projects we want to get done and how we'll prepare for the next quarter one." During one of our conversations, Kendra had just returned from their April off-site meeting. "It went so incredibly well! This week everyone is so energized, enthusiastic, and has this renewed vigor. Doing this every six months has made a huge impact," she states.

✓ **They write inspiration manifestos.** Kendra knows how important it is to lead with inspiration. She and her entire team write what they call inspiration manifestos, so that, as she explains, "once a day, or once a month, or whatever, we can lift up our heads and remember what it is we're doing here and why we're doing it." She was kind enough to share hers as director of client happiness:

> Ruby's Client Happiness Team is a League of Super Heroes and I am their leader, their mentor, their friend. I will make their time at Ruby the most fulfilling, inspiring, and challenging thing they've ever done, so when an opportunity for greatness comes along, we are ready. I will cultivate a place where the best of the best go to get even better. The world is waiting for us!
>
> I've got mine on a wall in my office and I refresh it every six months for the off-site. Then, we go around and read ours to each other—while we're drinking

mimosas. That's my "why." That's my why when it's hard for me to get up in the morning or I have a tough call to make or a tough situation to deal with. Those things happen in every job. I can look at my inspiration manifesto and remember that I'm creating a place where people who have higher standards, and who take pride in their work, and who have a passion for customer service can come, thrive, and be around other people like themselves.

✓ **They have a team manifesto.** Once everyone in the Client Happiness Department reads their own manifesto, they create one for the team. Kendra was kind enough to share that with me as well:

> We are a league of super heroes. We are leaders, advocates, and friends. We cultivate the right soil for ourselves and others to grow and thrive. We celebrate innovation, teamwork, and tacos. We believe happiness is a choice and that all people matter. We work with integrity and assume charitable intentions. We believe that the best answer is an elegant one. We are masters of sharing Ruby magic. Together we are pioneering the new frontier of world class service.

✓ **Ruby employees understand the Ruby Service Pyramid.** In fact, everyone at Ruby Receptionists knows that it is important to have a strong foundation in place if you want to have happy customers and a successful company. The Ruby Service Pyramid is based on the hierarchy of needs. So, you do the bottom things first and then reach for the top. It begins with *being prepared with the right infrastructure.* "That's our phone lines and our staffing. It's the building we work from. It's also our mission, vision, and values," elaborates Kendra. "That's our base from which we build everything. Next, we have to *do what we say we'll do.*"

Says Ruby CEO Jill Nelson, "Sending you a card congratulating you on your son's graduation isn't going to win us any points if we don't consistently answer your phone." On top of that, they *foster happiness, create experiences, give them what they don't even know they want,* and *make meaningful connections.* It's all driven by people and process.

✓ **Ruby Receptionists monitors key performance indicators.** "I look at our KPI's every single day. We have an indefinable quality of culture and inspiration at Ruby, and all that interpersonal stuff is really very important," says Kendra. "However, I also need data and hard numbers so I can be sure I'm on top of what's happening. For instance, most of our clients contact us through e-mail so we have e-mail queues. I need that wait time to be under 30 minutes because if a client e-mails and their interaction isn't assigned in 30 minutes, they'll be waiting a couple of hours for a response. That may be fine, but, I hope you know, Ruby isn't okay with fine." I do know. In fact, in all my years as a customer of Ruby Receptionist I don't think I've ever waited longer than 30 minutes for a response. Most of the time, it's more like five.

✓ **Ruby Receptionists restructures when needed.** Kendra and her client happiness team just changed the structure of their shifts to even out coverage. Instead of the former eight-hour shift, they've broken their day into three chunks. "We've got a 5 a.m. to 10 a.m., 10 a.m. to 2 p.m., and 2 p.m. to 6 p.m. We created work groups for each of those three time periods. They are accountable for client interactions that come in during those times. So, out of an eight-hour day, they are focusing on that queue for five hours. The rest of the time, they're finishing up interactions, spending time writing a note card, or sending a 'wow' gift to a client. *If you want your team to provide thoughtful and caring service, then you must give them room to be caring and thoughtful."*

✓ **Ruby Receptionists has a leadership book club.** Once a quarter, they read a book on leadership. "It's voluntary," says Kendra, "but if you participate, we'll make sure you have the book to read. Our client happiness team participates quite a bit."

Should you decide to start one of these, I can think of a book to make number one on your list (shameless promotion alert!).

Hotel at Auburn University

When asked to provide practical and tactical ideas for delivering red-carpet customer service, Hans Van Der Reijden said immediately, "The truth is to select the right people. You also need to have a culture that promotes, rewards, and encourages and inspires people to roll out the red carpet. You want to get to the point where this becomes second nature. It can only happen if you bring on people who have service as part of their DNA."

Sound familiar?

I asked him: "What is your system for ensuring you have the right people at the Hotel at Auburn University?"

✓ He responded, "What we specifically look for is a set of God-given talents and a demonstration that you really enjoy taking care of other people." Van Der Reijden, who began his career at Holland America and later spent 11 years opening properties for Ritz-Carlton, recalls, "As a young manager, I looked for people with a lot of skills, because that would cut down on training time and I could have them up and running very quickly. Over time, though, you learn that it's far more important to find people who have a positive attitude and enjoy taking care of people. The technical parts will come over time."

✓ While Hans was working for Ritz-Carlton, he worked in Bali and Indonesia for about five years. The Ritz-Carlton is a chain that is famous worldwide for its level of customer service:

> When we opened that hotel [in Bali], we specifically looked for employees who had never worked in the hotel business before. We didn't want them to come on board with bad habits that had been ingrained, that were now part the way they operated. The empathetic part came with the person walking through that door via a careful selection process. We trained them on things like: the fork goes left and the knife goes right, because people in the village in Bali don't typically eat with a knife or fork, so that's where you focus your time. Nobody took better care of our customers than the staff who had never worked in hospitality before because we were so focused on the customer.

Now Hans works in a university environment and has partnered with the Auburn University hospitality management program, where 65 percent of employees are students. "Many of them come here as freshmen and have never worked in a restaurant, or catering operation, or front desk situation before. But our customer satisfaction scores are through the roof. Why? Because we focus on selecting people who have that truly caring attitude."

✓ Orient people to your culture first. At Auburn University, no one goes into training for a job until they have had a full day of orientation. "We want to make sure each employee understands who we are from a philosophical point of view. If you don't do that first, they will be so focused on the technical piece. So we insist on orientation first. That way they understand whom they have decided to join. Once they have that, everything we ask them to do makes much more sense."

✓ Each day, at line-up, employees of The Hotel at Auburn University—as well as others within The Capella Hotel Group—spend time discussing their philosophy of *zeitgeist*. This German word translates roughly as "the spirit of the moment." It's one of the hotel's 24 service standards. Employees review a standard a day every 24 days. "It's about the power of repetition," says Hans. "On day 22, we have a hotel in China, one in Singapore, and one in Ireland talking about the exact same standard." Some of those standards include:

  ☐ We assist each other, stepping out of our primary duties to effectively provide service to our guest.

  ☐ Answer the telephone within three rings and with a smile in your voice. Use terminology that reflects The Hotel at Auburn University image. Do not screen calls. Avoid call transfers and placing guests on hold.

  ☐ Safety and security is everyone's responsibility. Know your role in an emergency situation and in protecting guest and hotel assets. Report unsafe conditions and security concerns immediately and correct them if possible.

☐ Escort guests until they are comfortable with directions or make visual contact with their destination. Do not point.

☐ Be respectful of our guests' personal time and privacy, delivering service that does not interrupt or interfere with our guests' activities. Never approach a guest to request a favor such as an autograph.

☐ Do not use casual, slangy words such as *hi, okay, no problem, guys,* or *folks.* Your goal is to create a worldly experience consistent with The Hotel at Auburn University image.

☐ Take pride in your appearance. Follow our grooming standards to ensure we convey a professional image.

☐ Be knowledgeable of the hotel's signature activities and unique offerings.

☐ As service professionals, we are always gracious and treat our guests and each other with respect and dignity.

✓ Hans elaborates, "I think that the biggest mistake we make as young managers is thinking that we are the only ones who can do line-up and that the employees really want to hear us talk every morning." I have to agree. His advice? "Ask your employees to give you examples of how they have brought the standard to life. It will give you the opportunity to recognize them for their good work and reinforce the expectation at the same time."

Northwell Health Has a Mission

When Sven Gierlinger took the job as vice president and chief experience officer for Northwell Health in New York, he asked his CEO not to expect anything for at least the first three months. "I didn't want to make any decisions or changes yet. I knew the most important thing for me to do was to build relationships," he relates. So, he visited every healthcare facility within the system, and either met with the leadership team or asked the executive director to walk him through the building. He asked them to share what they were proud of, what challenges they were facing, and where they wanted to go. "You can't change a culture without first building relationships," he notes.

Here are a few of the things he learned in the process that can help you get red-carpet ready:

✓ Step number one was to put together a governing structure to help improve the patient experience. The people of Northwell had always been passionate about improving service. However, while they had some success, it was inconsistent. Sven realized that, for the most part, this was because they had a decentralized approach to the customer experience. Each of the 20-plus hospitals and 400 physician practices pretty much did its own thing, with no core structure. Sven quickly realized that they didn't have a good forum for creating strategy, sharing the strategy, or sharing data. So he put together a "steering" committee composed of all the senior executives that had anything to do with patient experience. Now, every leader in each hospital knows that there is a commitment on the executive level to move the needle on patient experience scores in a positive direction. (Incidentally, their patient satisfaction scores and employee engagement scores were in exactly the same percentile when he started. No surprise there, as company culture, employee engagement, and customer happiness are directly linked.)

✓ In the hotel industry, a well-known rule is the 10/5 rule. It basically states that within 10 feet of another person (customer or coworker) you make eye contact and smile, and within 5 feet you provide a friendly greeting. "However," notes Sven, "often in a healthcare environment, the counters [at the front desk in the emergency room, for example] are so high and the desk area is so full of paperwork that you can't even see someone's eyes until they're about 3 feet in front of you." Sven has become passionate about changing the way desks are created, such that the reception and clinical team will be sitting at eye level with the customer and patient. In fact, as they open new clinics and make renovations in their current facilities, they are making this change.

✓ Sven continues, "The importance of leadership accountability cannot be overstated. Often, [other hospitals] promote a great nurse into a supervisory role without really delving into her leadership qualifications. To top it off, [they] don't really give [new promotions] enough training to be successful in their new role." Bingo! I wanted to stand up from my desk chair and applaud when he said this. Incidentally, this truth doesn't apply only to healthcare. It's critical that people promoted into leadership positions actually have the ability to step into that role, and that you give them the support they need to succeed.

✓ If you are serious about improving your customer experience, it's also imperative that you make it a top priority. Says Sven, "I asked our executive leaders these questions: 'What happens if our financial results are not where they need to be?' They easily answered, 'We get our team together, create an action plan, and get everything under control within a month.' Then I asked, 'What happens if we have an issue with clinical quality or a negative patient that has to be addressed?' Same answer: 'We jump into action, rally the troops, do a review, and put steps into place to make sure we never have a repeat performance.' Then I asked, 'What happens if our patient experience results are declining for three months in a row?' Silence. 'Do we have the same rigor in place? Do we take the same action steps we do in the other two areas?' The answer, unfortunately, is no. It hits people hard when you put it in that context. That's what we need to address in terms of leadership accountability. The same priority that's placed on financials and clinical events must be placed on customer service and patient experience in order for it to improve." Bravo!

✓ So how did Sven go about getting the leaders in his organization on board? In addition to sharing his own inspiring story (see Chapter 2), he presented each member of the executive steering committee with a book. The book is titled *Becoming the Most Customer-Centric Healthcare Organization in the U.S: How North Shore LIJ [now Northwell Health] Got to the 90th Percentile in Workforce Engagement & Patient Satisfaction*. The publishing date is 2017. He waited until the end of his first two-hour meeting with the exective steering committee to hand out the books. He told the team, "This is the most important book in healthcare and it's something we will learn a lot from. It's written by some of the highest authorities in patient satisfaction and healthcare." He asked them to open the book. The pages were blank. As they looked up at Sven with questions in their eyes, he simply stated, "We are writing this book together. We begin today." Goosebumps!

Since then, Sven and his group have handed the book out to others in their system. The recipients proudly display it. With every success, the comment is always made that "There's another chapter in the book!"

As Northwell Health has continued with this process, the physicians and other team members have become increasingly engaged. This is no longer the "flavor of the month"; this is a real culture change. "I'm proud to say we had our annual senior leadership retreat recently and a panel of physicians spent some time talking about what it means to lead patient satisfaction from their perspective. Because of their engagement, our CEO got up and proclaimed that we had reached a tipping point in the process."

"How did that make you feel?" I asked Sven.

"That was pretty cool," he replied.

KSL Resorts

Although this idea has already been shared, it's worth noting that Ed Eynon began his conversation with me by stating, "All great service starts with the right person. All service training begins with the right hire. In fact, frankly, your training can suffer unless you have the right person who could find a way to make it work without the training." I think you're starting to get the message!

With experience that ranges from his work with the Cheesecake Factory to the Salt Lake City Organizing Committee for the 2002 Winter Olympics, headed by former presidential candidate Mitt Romney, to his current position as the senior vice president of human resources for California-based KSL Resorts, Ed is full of ideas for building a solid foundation to support red-carpet customer service.

✓ "There are two parts to delivering exceptional service: the technical piece and the hospitality piece. You've got to get the technical piece right or you get punished. These are the areas people expect to be right. You don't get any great points for having them right, but you definitely get penalized if you don't have them right. However, if you have the hospitality piece right, that will earn you the return visits and referrals." Ed uses the metaphor of a guest visiting your home. "When your friends show up unannounced and ask to stay with you for three days, you might immediately go to the technical side of things: 'Do I have enough bedding? Is the house clean? Is there food in the fridge?' However, then you remember why they came to you in the first place. Unless they are complete freeloaders, they aren't here for the quality of the bed. They came because of the quality of human interaction. They came to make memories. There are clearly two parts to service and it's important to deliver on both of them. Yet, when push comes to shove, *hospitality trumps the technical every single time* [italics mine]."

✓ Ed and his team have spent a lot of time researching what works and what doesn't in terms of service standards, studying all the greats inside and outside the hotel industry to see if they shared common principles. Rather than train on several service standards, they have found that exceptional hospitality all boils down to four things. They call them the "Four Keys to Creating Guests for Life." At KSL Resorts, they are:

☐ Warmth: Genuine sincerity in every contact. A sincere welcome and a fond farewell.

☐ Personalization: Seek out the guest name and information. Use the guest's name and share it with others. Find out more about his or her visit.

☐ Awareness: Evaluate what is happening with the guest or situation. Observe and analyze in preparation for action.

☐ Proactivity: Take actions to delight the guest. Provide individualized service to the guest before being asked. Own and resolve service issues.

From a training perspective, everyone who is hired at KSL Resorts goes through a few hours of the "Four Keys" training.

✓ Then, adapting a tool used by the Ritz-Carlton, every team member is given a pocket card that combines the technical aspects of his or her specific position with the

104

hospitality side. These are called their KSL Standards of Excellence, and they are tailored to each specific position, chronologically going through the guest experience like a checklist that the person can easily understand. It also makes it easy for a manager to audit occasionally and give praise ("You're doing well on this") or coaching ("You missed a step").

✓ Always remember the value of your workforce. While Ed was preparing for the Salt Lake City Olympic Games, he had the opportunity to sit with the head of the Olympic Games that had been held in Norway. When asked for advice, the gentleman said, "I learned that the most important thing was getting the people part right. Getting the warmth and service that comes from people is critical. I used to think it was the technical matters. But if you get the timing and the scoring for the athletes right, and the transportation and the media center right, then you're good. However, when you get the hospitality, and the warmth, and anticipating needs right, that's what gets you to great." During Ed's tenure, Mitt Romney came in to head up the Salt Lake City Olympics in response to a worldwide scandal. "At first," says Ed, " he was all about dialing it back and getting to basics. He spent a lot of time thinking about the technical side, but, over time, shifted more and more to the people and hospitality side. I remember that after he had spent time in Sydney in 2000, he was interviewed by Matt Lauer and Katie Couric. They asked him what he had learned in Sydney that he would take back to Salt Lake. He said very simply: 'How important our workforce is to our success.'" At the time, NBC and the International Olympic Committee hailed the Salt Lake City Games as the best games ever held. At the very end, Mitt gathered everyone on the team together for a celebration event—complete with KC and the Sunshine Band. He told them, "A lot of people are going to take credit for these games, but as I have learned, our success comes from the value of the workforce."

Celebrate Customer Service Stories

With my passion for all things entertainment—theater and movies especially—I was thrilled to hear about a cinema chain that was focused on creating a red-carpet experience for its customers, off-screen and on. When I learned what Celebration Cinema, a family-owned theater exhibition company with 10 Cedars multiplexes in western and central Michigan, was doing to honor its local communities *and* teach customer service principles at the same time, I couldn't wait to share it with you.

✓ "We love telling stories and we believe storytelling informs culture," shares Emily Loeks, director of community affairs at Celebration Cinema. "We think that is true with the movies that we put on our screens, but also that it's the way the very best teachers have operated throughout history. So we thought that maybe one of the most meaningful ways to get our employees to absorb the level of service we want them to provide was to tell stories about the places that inspire us." So they armed every single one of their 600 to 700 employees with the ability to carry around a free movie pass. Whenever they experience what we define as "celebrated service" from another business in the community, they thank the service provider with a free movie pass. "The only requirement for our staff is that they come back to a staff meeting or to the employee break room and share the story with others," she relates. "People set the bar pretty high. You'd think the passes would be flying out the doors. But our team holds a very high bar for what they believe is truly 'celebrated service.' Oftentimes, though, it's the basics. The kids [Celebration Cinema employees] are remembered by name or they get looked in the eyes and greeted well. Sometimes it's that when an order comes out wrong, the staff member [goes] the extra mile to correct it and add a little something special." Emily and the Celebration Cinema leadership team found that while their employees were telling stories about businesses that were very different from their industry, they were absorbing things that are very relevant to the service Celebration Cinema aspires to provide each other and their guests. Brilliant!

✓ "The whole process leads to every employee in our company having the ability to make a nomination of a business each year. They nominate organizations that are consistently getting it right and are a model we can learn from." The employees reach out to their nominees, asking if they'd like to participate in a campaign that Celebration Cinema runs each year to champion and celebrate businesses that provide great service. If they accept the nomination, the team at Celebration Cinema goes through a process to determine 10 businesses they feel they'd be proud to endorse and share as champions within the community. Says Emily, "We leverage our whole theater circuit— our screens, employees, and media relationships—to tell their stories and share what it is we love about them. For a stretch of two weeks we engage the whole community in a public vote to determine who the Celebration Service Award Champion will be each year. We'd be proud to champion any of the 10 businesses, but there is only one winner," she adds. For that business, the team at Celebration Cinema interviews team members on film and creates a 30-second segment that is shown on the company's movie screens all year long. They also share the story on their social media channels, throw a movie party for their staff members, and provide them with passes they can hand out to guests or employees as the occasion arises. "The number-one goal for the campaign," stresses Emily, "is to use this kind of storytelling to improve the level of service we give [to] each other and our guests. And there's an added, long-lasting benefit: Some of our team members advance into positions of leadership and management. For most, however, this is a high school or college job. You don't carry making popcorn with you to a next employment opportunity, but we felt like there are a couple of things we can do as a theater company that are valuable to carry on. One of those things is to do a really great job empowering our employees and building a culture of celebrated service. Maybe, over time, other companies in the region will realize that someone who came from Celebration is somebody who has the service DNA they are seeking." I wouldn't be surprised!

✓ Another strategy the company uses is to practice business transparency and open-book finance. Every Celebration Cinema employee has the ability to see most of the key metrics—both numerical and cultural—that sustain the health of Celebration Cinema's business. (Cultural metrics includes things like customer comments, peer-to-peer recognition, and something called the SSEXI score [superior shared experience index], which is similar to the net promotor score mentioned later in this chapter.) Emily has heard from many employees that seeing these figures in black and white was eye opening and even shocking. "They never understood the numbers behind what they were doing. Until they saw them, they never would have guessed how much impact they had on our bottom line. They assumed the margins were much bigger and that a little bit here or there didn't make a difference. Now they realize that being attentive to the details and getting customers to return actually makes or breaks businesses."

You'll read more about Celebration Cinema in future chapters. For now, consider how much that kind of powerful storytelling and community involvement could teach *your* employees about the power of exceptional service.

Communicate Your Core Values

As you can see, most organizations whose team members become known for delivering an extraordinary customer experience begin with strong core values. However, it's not as important to have them as it is to communicate them and live them every day. Here are 10 quick ways you can consistently communicate your core values. You can download the full report for free by visiting our Website at *www.redcarpetlearning.com*.

1. **Lead by example.** Your employees are watching you. Remember the old saying that actions speak louder than words.

2. **Have a values relaunch.** If you've had them for a while but no one remembers what they are, create a little hoopla around them and reignite commitment to your values.

3. **Use your company's core values to make decisions.** Yes, every decision.

4. **Use your organization's core values to hire the right people.** Yes, every person.

5. **Talk about your business's core values on day one.** No new hire should get through the first day without knowing your company's core values.

6. **Promote a value of the month.** Or day, or week.

7. **Include your core values in your job descriptions and performance reviews.** You want team members who are aligned with your organizational values.

8. **Create rituals that keep your core values at the forefront.** Workplace rituals anchor them in the minds of your employees.

9. **Weave your core values into your current traditions.** Why reinvent the wheel?

10. **Tell stories worth sharing that tie into your core values.** Stories tap into emotions that cause people to think and act differently. Include your core values in your job descriptions and performance reviews.

Ditch the Performance Reviews

Yes, you read that right—ditch the reviews! Here's why: If you're like many leaders, you probably have a pile of employee performance reviews backed up on your to-do list. A few years ago, the leadership team at Garden Spot Village, a residential living community in New Holland, Pennsylvania, found themselves in exactly that position. It was the end of June and they were scrambling to get all the reviews done in the last two weeks before the end of the fiscal year. They began to question the need for traditional performance reviews, and asked, "Is there a better way?" The answer, it turns out, was yes! They replaced the traditional model, the one in which a manager gives her employee a score once a year, with very little feedback in between, with a coaching program.

✓ At the beginning of the fiscal year, every team member sits down with a coach. Instead of having objectives imposed on them by the boss, team members work with their coaches to set their own goals. Their aspirations can be both personal and professional. For instance, one team member had a goal to buy her first house. Her coach worked with her to help her get to the point where she could. As CMO Scott Miller says, "This program extends beyond the borders of our organization."

✓ Each participant meets formally with his or her coach three times a year. Rather than using a traditional rating scale, team members place an X alongside a bar to designate how far along they are toward their goals. They are encouraged to simply "move the needle to the right." Says Scott, "One social worker enthusiastically shared with me that she accomplished more of her goals in one year of coaching than she had in the previous five years she'd worked at Garden Spot Village."

ProSportsLives.com

Gena Pitts is the publisher and editor-in-chief for *Pro Sports Lives* magazine, a publication that caters to the families of professional athletes, coaches, sports executives, and celebrities in the sports entertainment industry. She feels strongly about the need to train one's team on the right way to deliver customer service. "Employers must stop assuming that their team members know how to deliver red-carpet service and provide them with the tools they need to learn," states Gena.

✓ She's a fan of training that's a bit out of the box. "Thanks to technology, we've become a society of visual learners," she asserts. So she finds visually appealing and interesting ways to teach her team members how to address the needs of her customers. For instance, for one training program, Gena hired a troupe of actors to role-play the needs of a family and portray the right and wrong way to handle the situation. "Allowing my team members to see how it feels to be on the other side of the fence gave them the perspective needed to provide exceptional customer service," she observes.

Morale on the Movie Set

I found Shruti Ganguly, vice president of television and video for *Nylon* magazine, because she produced a fun and effective employee morale-booster and viral video called *The $100.00 Challenge.* You'll read more about it in Chapter 6. In the meantime, Shruti, who is also a producer and director of several independent and feature films such as *The Color of Time* (starring James Franco, Mila Kunas, and Jessica Chastain), has many valuable suggestions when it comes to creating an environment where people thrive.

✓ **Discover the "why":** "Ultimately," says Shruti, "I want to know why my team wakes up and comes to work. What does this do for them beyond getting a paycheck? It's on me to create an environment where they feel inspired, can grow, and feel a part of something bigger."

✓ **Be flexible with outside interests:** There's no doubt about it. The world is changing, and the new generation does not look at work the same way that previous generations did. It's important to value the whole person and recognize what each team member brings to the table. Says Shruti, "When I joined *Nylon,* I also had five movies going into production, a TV deal, and was directing videos.

Rather than ask me to stop and focus on the one job, my other commitments were encouraged and celebrated. That's what I love about my boss [Paul Greenberg]. One element of my work feeds another and he welcomes that!"

✓ **Squash negativity:** Shruti, who has a master's of degree in business administration as well as a master's in film, knows that her business degree accounts for much of her success when producing movies. "When I'm producing," she says, "I'm very sensitive to vibes and energy. I can always tell if there's some form of negativity and I immediately research where it's coming from. When you're dealing with actors who are going to wear the 'skin' of another character, they're making themselves pretty vulnerable. You want to create a place where you can get the best performances. If you have someone with a bad attitude nearby, that really affects performance and can make or break a film. I'm very particular about managing what's going on under the surface." When asked how she handles it, Shruti responds, "I do a little research to find out what's going on and I start with a conversation with the person. The amount of sternness depends on the context. If someone really isn't doing his job, I remind him why we're here and what needs to happen. If the employee is on board, great! If not, I need to find another solution." Regardless of the work setting, this rings true. One negative person can derail your efforts to create a red-carpet ready workplace. It's best to deal with it before the sequel.

The WOWplace Rules

My good friend and international speaker Sandy Geroux is the author of *Turn Your Workplace Into a WOWplace! 5 Rules for Going From OW! to*

WOW! and the founder of WOWplace International: *www.wowplace.com.* She has a lot of wisdom to share about what makes a company a great place to work:

✓ **Build a WOWplace instead of a workplace.** What is a WOWplace? According to Sandy, "A workplace is a place where employees have to go because they make a paycheck. A WOWplace is a place where people love to go because they make a difference." Here's her advice for laying a foundation that will inspire and empower your team to deliver service that wows. She calls them The WOWplace Rules:

  ☐ **A WOWplace is safe:** "In other words, it's a place where people feel comfortable sharing their ideas and suggestions because they will be welcomed and appreciated," Sandy explains.

  ☐ **A WOWplace is respectful:** "Respect isn't given because of a title, but because it is earned and re-earned every single day," says Sandy.

  ☐ **A WOWplace is human...not humanoid:** "The people in a WOWplace really care about people. They get to know each other. Leaders in a WOWplace know that their people will never go to the wall for someone they don't know and respect," explains Sandy.

  ☐ **A WOWplace is innovative, creative, and fun:** "For people to think outside the box, there has to be a box. That's the structure and the starting point. Then, you have to foster an environment where those who work there can be creative. The new 'coffeehouse generation' won't be able to generate ideas in an empty conference room with a long table. Give them a place where they can feel comfortable sharing their knowledge," Sandy encourages.

☐ **A WOWplace is rewarding:** "The rewards are emotional, financial, inspiring, personal, and intrinsic. They come from leaders and they come from each other," Sandy elaborates.

Great guidelines for a workplace that wows!

Great Service Is Habit Forming

They say it take between 21 and 30 days to make a habit. You can find wonderfully simple 30-day programs for your team members at *www.avanoo.com*. Additionally, I have at least two 30-day customer service training programs for sale on my site. You can also find programs on leadership, time management, and even personal development.

Know your Net Promoter Score

As you lay the foundation for improving the customer experience, it's important to know the results you're shooting for. There are a variety of metrics you can set and share with your team to ensure your efforts are headed in the right direction.

One such metric is your Net Promoter Score. Our director of delight, Rachel Street, had the opportunity to speak with Richard Owen, author of the book *Answering the Ultimate Question: How Net Promoter Can Transform Your Business* and one of the codevelopers of the Net Promoter Score and the Net Promoter System, along with Laura Brooks and Fred Reichheld. Says Richard, "The Net Promoter Score was originally conceived as a metric about 10 or so years ago. It was based on research that indicated that there is, in fact, a proven linkage between customer loyalty and financial performance."

✓ By implementing the Net Promoter Score metric as part of your red-carpet readiness, in essence you will be measuring the number of raving fans you have. The metric is based on the notion of whether your customers would recommend your products and services to somebody else. The scale ranges from 0 to 10. Those who give you a 9 or 10 are called Promoters (your raving fans). Those who give you a 7 or an 8 are called Passives (they like you okay, but they aren't necessarily advocates of your organization). Those who give you a 0 to 6 are called Detractors. "The Net Promoter Score," explains Richard, "really measures the customer's overall relationship with your brand as opposed to one specific experience you might have had with them. The reason it's divided up this way is that, as it turns out, Promoters, Passives, and Detractors all behave very differently when it comes to future purchasing intent, profitability, and lifetime value. So this is a quantifiable metric that is directly tied to financial performance. However, there's another benefit to the Net Promoter Score methodology," adds Richard. "The concept is very easy to communicate. So it helps organizational leaders get their team members engaged and excited."

Can You Handle the Truth?

Finally, if you're going to inspire your team to roll out the red carpet for your customers, just say no to diva behavior and rock-star delusions of grandeur. The biggest star on the lot must be the most gracious and the most appreciative if you want others to follow you down the red-carpet road.

Debbie Ley, co-owner of Something New for I Do, a PR/marketing company and unique resource for brides who want to brand their wedding, saw this firsthand when her event venue was used to house Tom Cruise's green room while he was filming *Mena* in her city of Ball Ground, Georgia. "You'd think a megawatt celebrity like him would require high-profile star treatment," said Debbie. Not so in this case. "They put up a small tent that was around 10 feet by 20 feet. Inside was a sofa, some chairs, a makeup table, and a little fridge with some bottled water. No big demands and very unpretentious. It was simple and he was extremely gracious."

The cast and crew of *Mena* spent weeks filming in Ball Ground, Georgia, and it became commonplace for Debbie and her partners to see Tom and the other actors walking outside her window. "He was very hands-on, often watching the monitors when they finished filming a scene and wanting to ensure he got it just right," she says. "When he wasn't acting, for the most part, he was talking with the

crew and to fellow actors, and waving to the fans nearby. He was very even keel and absolutely kind and courteous the entire time. If he had time, when they finished filming, he spent time with the fans outside, thanking them for welcoming the cast and crew into their town." (The people of Ball Ground clearly loved it, as evidenced by the many comments and photos on their self-launched Facebook page "Cruisin' Ball Ground.")

Debbie's real thrill came when they asked to film a scene inside her venue. "They said Tom's character was going to kick the door open and walk in with suitcases full of money. At first they sent his double, but then the door flew open and it was Tom himself. Each time he would make little jokes, like 'I don't usually make an entrance like this,' or promising he wouldn't be too hard on our door." At one point a crew member asked them to leave, but Tom overruled and invited them to stay and watch.

After they wrapped the scene, he chatted and posed for pictures with Debbie and her friends, thanking them for their space and exclaiming on what a great experience they were having in Ball Ground. "Again," said Debbie, "not demanding at all. Gracious and charming. That's the Tom Cruise brand."

She's right. Mr. Cruise has certainly had his share of media troubles, but one thing has always stayed consistent. Those who work with him have been known to say that he makes you want to work harder because he works so hard himself. He knows the names of all the crew members and does what he can to keep morale up on the set. He's legendary for showing up hours before a premiere and staying later so he can spend more time with the fans.

Sadly, I've met CEOs who walk past the very employees who serve their customers without a smile or a hello. Trust me, it's noticed. And it doesn't build morale or loyalty. It destroys it. Here are a few ways to help build morale in your company:

✓ Spend time out and about with your "cast" and "crew." Walk the floor of your building and get to know your employees. Be gracious, humble, and appreciative. Joke around with them. Have fun. If your team members see that you expect as much of yourself as you do of them, that you are kind and caring, and that you appreciate the work they do, they may just follow you anywhere.

Are you red-carpet ready? Great! Let's go make some movie moments!

Questions for Discussion

- What must we do to become red-carpet ready?
- Do we have the right people in the right roles?
- Are we orienting people to our culture? Are we giving our team the tools they need to succeed?

CHAPTER FOUR

Make "Movie Moments"

Do you remember when Danny traded his leather jacket for a letterman's sweater in the movie *Grease*, only to be floored when Sandy showed up in leather and big hair, and they flew off the shiny red car to live happily ever after? Or the time when Rocky Balboa ran up the steps of the Philadelphia Art Museum in *Rocky*? Or when Luke Skywalker discovered the identity of his father in *The Empire Strikes Back*? If you saw any of these movies, these are moments that you'll remember forever. You've probably talked about them with your friends. Word of mouth (WOM) is one of the reasons why those movies were so successful. Think about it. If you saw *The Sixth Sense*, you know there is a moment in that movie that takes you completely by surprise and changes the entire experience for you. It's the moment that made you tell your friends, "You *have* to see *The Sixth Sense!*"

What if you could create those kinds of moments for your customers? Moments that take them completely by surprise and make them see you in a new light. Moments that incite an emotional response. Moments that cause them to tell their friends, "You have to see what they're doing over at [your company]." I call these "movie moments." The leaders of the company I discuss next call it "practicing WOWism."

Whether you call them "movie moments," "WOWisms," or "moments that surprise and delight," creating them may earn you not only loyal fans but a virtual sales force for your business.

Practice WOWism

Remember the days when you called a company and an honest-to-goodness, live person answered the phone? Remember when your calls were answered by cheerful, upbeat receptionists who would go the extra mile to get you the answers you were seeking? Do you recall a time when you made meaningful connections with people who weren't named Siri? If you're like most people (at least the Gen X-ers and the Baby Boomers), you long for those days. Enter Ruby Receptionists.

Jill Nelson, the CEO and visionary behind this growing company, founded Ruby Receptionists in 2003 with the dream of taking businesses back to the time when friendly, cheerful, and professional call answering was the norm. Her ideal clients are business owners who can't always answer their own phones but want to give their customers a more personal connection than an automated, computer-generated caller response service.

Nelson began her company in a small sculptor's studio in Portland, Oregon. She now has more than 100 team members, two offices, and a wall full of awards. Ruby Receptionists is a five-time Fastest Growing Company award winner in Oregon. In 2012, Ruby Receptionists was named the #1 Small Company to Work for by *Fortune Magazine*. In 2009, one of the worst years of the recession, Ruby Receptionists doubled in size due to referrals from their customers.

My company, Red-Carpet Learning Systems, Inc., is a long-time customer of Ruby Receptionists (affectionately known as "Call Ruby"). I hired them because my team is scattered all over the country. I travel a great deal, and wanted my phone answered by a friendly, live person who could immediately connect to us anywhere. We continue to use Ruby Receptionists because they deliver what they promise. Our calls are answered quickly and professionally by an enthusiastic, upbeat person. The transfer of calls is seamless. If a call is for me, and I'm unavailable, the caller is given several options for leaving a message, and I am immediately notified. When I tell them I'm unavailable, every Ruby Receptionist gets that message and knows exactly what to tell callers. They follow everything up with an immediate e-mail so we are always in the loop and never miss a call. They even call people back with information. If their computer system goes down (which is extremely rare), they immediately e-mail us and keep us continually updated until it is all working again. In short, I continue to use Ruby Receptionists because they nail the basics. Remember the foundation of the Ruby Pyramid from Chapter Three?

My team and I have become advocates (raving fans) for our "Rubies" because they continually surprise and delight us with unexpected "movie moments" or "WOWisms" at every turn. Like most organizations that exude a red-carpet-service culture, everything Ruby does stems from their core values:

- Foster happiness.
- Practice WOWism.
- Create community.
- Innovate.
- Grow.

You'll learn more about Ruby Receptionists in other parts of this book. For the purposes of this chapter, let's focus on their value of "practice WOWism." Here are three specific ways in which I've personally seen this in action:

✓ After a particularly tough and exhausting morning of travel, I e-mailed the "Rubies" to let them know I was taking the rest of the day off and to ask them to take messages. As usual, I immediately received a cheerful e-mail reply from Clarice, one of their receptionists, who assured me they would gladly do so. Perfect! What I didn't expect was the package I received from Clarice in the mail three days later. It was filled with dog treats. Yes, dog treats, and a little picture frame with a sweet little Maltese puppy at the top. It was a "movie moment" for me and for my Maltese pup. How Clarice knew I had a Maltese, I'll never know for sure. I suspect she did a little research on my Facebook page. Snowball has since moved on to another dimension, but while she was with us she was one of Call Ruby's biggest fans!

✓ When I returned home from having a dream-come-true experience of sitting in bleachers on the red carpet for the annual Academy Awards, a package was delivered to my door. It contained a gold plastic statue, with a note from receptionists Dallas and Kate that read, "Just in case you didn't win anything at the Oscars, we want you to know you're a winner in our book."

✓ For several years, Ruby Receptionists sent a small desk calendar at the end of each year for the following year. I would pass it on to my husband, Jim, who happily placed it by his computer and used it regularly. One year, the calendar never arrived. I reached out to Jill Holmes, Ruby Receptionists' problem solver and chief happiness maker. She replied that, sadly, they had decided not to give out calendars this year. However, a few weeks later a different desk calendar arrived in the mail. The card, which had Jim's name on it, expressed regret that the calendar didn't have the Ruby branding but hoped that he would find it useful. Jill stocked up on desk calendars so she was ready to practice WOWism for clients who missed the Ruby calendars.

We aren't the only Ruby clients to benefit from these types of "movie moments." In fact, the leaders at Ruby Receptionists have deliberately set up systems so their team members are empowered to take action to surprise and delight every customer. Each "Ruby" has access to an account so that, when inspiration strikes, any one of them can send an inexpensive, unexpected gift to the client. They also have a gifting station at each office. At any time throughout the day, you might find a "Ruby" wrapping a treat in the provided paper, adding a colorful ribbon, and packing it in a box with a card included.

Founder Jill Nelson and the leaders at Ruby Receptionists understand that in order to roll out the red carpet for your customers, you must first roll it out for your team members. To that end, any Ruby team member can request $50 to put on a WOWism event for the rest of the team. Ruby Receptionists are true masters at Practicing WOWism and making movie moments. Here are some examples of people in other organizations who are unexpectedly delighting their customers as well.

The Answer Is Yes! The Question Is "How?"

The answer is yes! The question is "how?" That was the premise Rick Salmeron, owner of Salmeron Financial, was acting on when he decided to deliver ice cream to his customers, nation-wide, for one week in the middle of July. "I'm not only in the financial services business," says Rick, "but also in the client experience business."

✓ Based in Dallas, Texas, Rick is no stranger to mind-numbing July heat. Hoping to create some buzz for his business, he had a choice between another ad in the newspaper or capitalizing on social media by making "movie moments" for his customers. He sent out 200 e-mails to clients, prospects, and centers of influence. It read: "Have you seen the weather forecast? It's *hot* out there! We want to help you beat the heat. Simply respond to this email and we will have ice cream delivered to your door."

✓ Though most of the e-mails were sent to people in Dallas or Houston, Rick reached out to people coast to coast. He put the offer on his Facebook page and tweeted it a few times. Says Rick, "I honestly was going on blind faith. I had no idea how I would get it done. However, I thought I'd see who responded and figure it all out as I went along."

Rick had more 120 scoops of ice cream delivered all over the country that week. Working with local ice cream shops, he had people in Oregon, Oklahoma, Florida, Ohio, and North Carolina opening their front doors to find a smiling person delivering their ice cream. Locally, he was able to deliver some himself. People far and wide took selfies

with their ice cream scoops and posted them on Facebook. Comments Rick, "For less money than it would have cost me to take out an ad, I received more social media love, handwritten notes, and brand awareness than ever before. Because I stepped out of my comfort zone, my red carpet is wider and longer than ever. Each quarter, I make a point to market my services creatively, and no longer restrict my imagination."

✓ When David Mendes and his date stopped by a Chicago restaurant for a late evening dinner, initially they were told, "We're closed!" by the manager. They turned away disappointed, ready to head in a different direction. Then, the same manager popped his head back outside and said, "You know what? Come on in." He offered them a seat and proceeded to have his staff bring out all the leftover appetizers and entrees in the kitchen. David and his date had the place to themselves and enjoyed a tremendous feast while the staff, cleaning up around them, entertained them with anecdotes and conversation. A moment that could have resulted in two lost customers became a "movie moment" that turned David and his date into advocates for the restaurant. "I personally have brought no less than 30 different friends to dine there due to that one experience," says David.

✓ Moving into a retirement community can be stressful, both for the new resident and for family members. When one family was moving their mom from the hospital into The Remington Club in San Diego, California, the experience was fraught with difficulties. By the time move-in day finally arrived, the woman's two sons were exhausted. When the salesperson at The Remington Club asked if there was anything else he could do, one of the sons replied, "Unless you have a six pack of cold beer, I think you've done everything you can." They all shared a laugh. Then, the salesperson ran across the street and returned, to the astonishment and delight of the two men, with a cold six pack.

✓ "I try to make my team fully understand that we really only have a couple of rules," says Michael Colvin, director of event services at Durham Performing Arts Center. "One is that you have to have a ticket to see the show. Other than that, there aren't a lot of rules. If someone asks for something we don't normally do, as long as it's not a safety issue or could potentially take away from another guest experience, we try to accommodate them. So, for instance, when people began to ask us about putting gifts on the seat of a loved one, our initial reaction was that it wasn't a good idea. Then we thought about it. Why not? As long as they understand we're not responsible if it disappears, there's no harm. It's all about making our customer feel good. We try not to say no. One of our goals at DPAC is to eliminate that word from the vocabulary and check on something. If we can, we'll do it!"

Unexpected Treats

✓ Does your car windshield need a wash? Stop by the drive-through at Western State Bank in Devils Lake, North Dakota, and you might just find bank tellers outside ready to serve. It's called "Wild Wednesdays at Western State Bank." Tellers and other bank employees take half-hour shifts for two hours, washing the windshields of their customers, passing out tickets for door prizes, and delivering tasty treats to your car door.

✔ Many hotels now serve freshly baked cookies in the lobby each evening. The Crowne Plaza, in Lansing, Michigan, takes it a step further by delivering milk and cookies to your room. Every guest is offered cookies, milk, and a healthy option each night. You don't even have to leave the comfort of your room to get them.

✔ When new residents move in to The Mather, an upscale retirement community in Chicago, Illinois, they are given the royal treatment in the following ways:

  ☐ An orange carpet is rolled out to welcome them. (The Mather's signature color is orange, not red.)
  ☐ The resident's favorite snacks are in a basket on the table and stocked in the refrigerator.
  ☐ The resident's favorite song can be heard coming out of the CD player.
  ☐ Key staff members leave handwritten welcome notes.

I've personally received the "orange carpet" treatment from Mather LifeWays, the company that owns The Mather, in the following ways:

  ☐ Upon arriving in my guest apartment, in addition to all the amenities listed above, there was a framed document that told me of all the best places in the country to go hiking. Somehow, they had discovered my love of hiking and personalized my room. Wow! Double wow when I entered my room the next evening to find that the document had been changed. It now read "Best Snacks to Bring When Hiking." Each night of my stay there was something new, all tied to my love of hiking.
  ☐ If you read my first book, *The Celebrity Experience*, you might remember the story of HUB Plumbing and

Mechanical of Boston, Massachusetts. One of the many ways they created "surprise and delight moments" at the time was to swap out their customers' toilet paper rolls and replace them with a roll bearing the HUB plumbing logo. I spoke of this anecdote in my presentation, and Mary Leary, the CEO of Mather LifeWays, sent a team member up to replace my white toilet paper roll with a bright orange one. Imagine my surprise!

□ When our director of delight, Rachel Street, told the team at The Mather that I still had a crush on my "first love" David Cassidy, they gave me the typical orange-carpet treatment by making sure his signature song was playing in my guest apartment when I entered. However, the real "movie moment" came a few days later. Just as I opened my mouth to begin my presentation, a fourth of the audience stood up wearing homemade David Cassidy masks.

✓ The Hampton Inn of Ephrata, Pennsylvania, creates a "movie moment" for one guest each day by naming that person the "Guest of the Day." They are randomly selected and surprised with a sign in the lobby, a premier parking spot, free gifts, and hotel upgrades.

✓ Scan My Photos, founded in 1990, is a photo, slide, and negative scanning service. "It's a very emotional business," says Mitch Goldstone, president and CEO. "People send in their decades and generations of nostalgic photos to be digitized and preserved, as well as shared on social media. In the past, we did all of the traditional marketing and advertising. But I realized that this business was so emotional that we wanted to come up with something really unique to help get the word out. So we stopped all advertising, all marketing, everything." Instead they surprise their customers with flowers. In some cases, the flowers cost as much as the order or even more. "Customers include all types of messages about the photos and themselves. If it's a special 50th anniversary celebration or a sad event, such as a memorial, we send the appropriate bouquet ...along with a personalized message on the card." They choose random customers based on analytics from their software. It's based more on the story than the cost of sale. "We've had customers place $20 orders for a photo scan and they get a $100 floral arrangement." The response from customers, as you might imagine, has been spectacular. "It's a total surprise to them," says Mitch. "Each morning, I have a series of messages from the prior day, including comments from customers. They are wonderful. It engages them and sparks conversation. Many people ask how I can afford to do it. My response is, *I can't afford not to*. There's value—both emotional and economical—in making someone's day. Most importantly, it has to come right from the heart." As Mitch spoke to me, I could tell he was truly touched by how happy his customers were with the surprise. At the same time, I had to ask: "How has this affected your bottom line?" "It funds itself," he said. "Each bouquet or basket averages about $70. We're generating several thousand dollars in sales through referrals without advertising. So, if you're spending $70 and you're making $1,500 to $2,000, that's pretty great."

✓ When my husband and I stayed at the Gaylord Opryland in Nashville, Tennessee, we found ourselves running short on coffee. We ran down to the gift store to see if they had any. They did not. The cashier asked, "Wasn't there coffee in your room?" "Yes," I replied, "but we drink a lot of coffee and it's already gone. That's okay, we'll wait until morning." Now, let me start by telling you that the Gaylord Opryland Celebrity Services Department was heavily featured in my first book. So at that time, there was a handful of people who knew me and my husband, Jim. Though I absolutely never expected this, they would often give us the star treatment while we were there. However, this cashier didn't know us from Adam. That's why we were even more blown away when we returned to our room and found a box of coffee packets with all the fixings sitting on the counter. One of the Gaylord Opryland's service basics is "discover and delight." On that day, that cashier certainly did both.

Personalize, Surprise, and Delight

✓ Joni Cohen, a magazine editor turned consultant, works with small businesses to help them gain media exposure. When she wants to send a thank you or celebrate someone's special occasion, she sends them a personalized ice cream package. She buys them from eCreamery.com. Each pint is personalized with the recipient's name or a special message. When asked about her recipient's reaction, Joni responds, "They love it! Nobody buys four pints of ice cream for themselves. When it arrives, it's like an instant party!"

✓ Whenever new residents move into Leisure Park Retirement Community in Lakewood, New Jersey, they receive personalized welcome gifts with a Mylar balloon attached. For instance, one gentleman was a coin collector, so his gift was a couple of special coins. A resident who loves to read received a book, and another who loves to paint received a gift certificate for an art class. The key to the company's personalization is the gifting closet. Leisure Park Retirement Community keeps a closet stocked with small gifts in specific categories. They have gifts for book lovers, pet lovers, veterans, art lovers, grandparents, and sports lovers. They have Mylar balloons that celebrate almost every sports team and especially (being in New Jersey) the Yankees. The gifting closet facilitates easy personalization whenever they want to surprise and delight a new resident—or anyone!

✓ Rick Salmeron of Salmeron Financial is, like me, a customer of Ruby Receptionists. Also pleased with their level of service, Rick surprised the "Rubies" with delicious cookies personalized with their logo.

✓ To celebrate his 50th birthday, Scott Verissimo booked himself on a trip he'd been dreaming of for years: a transatlantic crossing on the *Queen Mary 2*. As you might expect, a voyage on a luxury ship such as this is all about red-carpet treatment. When Scott boarded the *Queen Mary 2*, the crew took his picture, presumably for security purposes. Apparently, there are other ways that photo is used, as well. Says Scott, "When I walked into the dining room I was greeted by name by the maîtres, by my main waiter, by the busboy, and by the wine steward. That greeting totally knocked my socks off! It was a seemingly small gesture that had a *huge* impact on me. I instantly felt at home and very, very special."

✓ Los Angeles-based Realtor Chantay Bridges loves to make "movie moments" for her clients. Some examples:

☐ Two potential clients got the purple carpet treatment (their favorite color), a limo ride, special drinks, and VIP seats to the circus as a combination treat and birthday surprise.

☐ She often sends little gifts, meaningful to the recipient, just to let them know she's thinking of them. Lucky clients have received cupcakes, spa gift cards, PetSmart cards, and strawberries dipped in chocolate.

☐ Chantay even sponsored a high-tea baby shower for one of her real estate clients who was having her first child.

☐ She has surprised multiple individuals, including giving a college student her very own home makeover.

How does all of this effort affect business? "I do receive a lot of referrals," says Chantay, "and for that I am grateful. Even when the market fluctuates, it has not stopped the telephone from ringing. It's all about the relationships I'm building by caring beyond the sale."

✓ Jamie Bennett is a concierge and the owner of a lifestyle management company that serves primarily high-net-worth individuals. "In my line of business, anticipating client needs is imperative," says Jamie. A year or so ago, Jamie's colleague introduced her to an executive who was interested in using her services. One of the first assignments was to purchase a Christmas tree and decorate it, as he hadn't had one in a while. "When I inquired as to my client's favorite colors, he said he didn't have any. After some research, my team and I discovered that he was a member of a well-known fraternity. We purchased a 12-foot tree and decorated it in the client's fraternity colors. We were even able to have customized bulbs bearing the fraternity logo. The client was beyond pleased. Jamie notes, "He's still my client almost two years later!"

✓ One of Jamie's expert tips for ensuring you personalize, surprise, and delight is to pay special attention to *every little detail* the client reveals about themselves. "When I'm out of their sight, I will quickly grab a pen and notepad and scribble down anything that might be useful later. What are their preferences, their wishes, and their dislikes? Then I have that information for the time when an opportunity to amaze and astonish them arises."

✓ The team at Talent Plus celebrates their customers' accomplishments by sending videos. Says cofounder Kimberly Rath, "If they've won Great Places to Work in their city or are having an anniversary or something, we will all get together and do a quick video and send it their way. People love the little videos!"

Memories in the Making

✓ Diane McGauley and her family will never forget the kindness of a nurse at Suncoast Hospice of Florida. When it became clear that her brother-in-law would soon pass away in the hospice house where he was staying without the chance to say good-bye to his beloved horse, the nurse knew something had to be done. She made arrangements for the horse to be brought to the window of his room so he could say good-bye for the last time. Diane and her family will remember and treasure this unexpected gesture for years to come.

Emily Loeks, director of community affairs for Celebration Cinema, shared this story:

About a year or so ago, there was a young woman facing enormous medical concerns. Her family wanted to give her a movie experience. She had never had one. We rolled out the red carpet for her. Her brother served as her valet. This young girl was probably 10 or 11 years old and she looked about 5 or 6 because of having gone through surgeries her entire life. She was wearing a full-length gown and carrying an evening bag. She had her whole neighborhood of kids and her family's closest friends in tow. They all showed up in limousines, and she just marched right into the theater with as much gallantry as I've ever seen. This was part of the final year of her life and this was a moment she always wanted to have happen. We love to do things like that because we can!

One of the loveliest ways to enjoy living in Asheville, North Carolina, is getting an annual pass to the Biltmore Estate, an imposing and majestic castle built by George Vanderbilt on 8,000 acres of absolutely gorgeous grounds. On the property is the Inn at Biltmore, an elegant four-star hotel with luxury amenities, overlooking sweeping mountain views. Here are two ways the Inn provides exceptional service to guests:

- ✓ You're greeted by the bellman as you walk inside the lobby, enjoying the impeccable service and the live piano music. You'll feel as you just stepped into a scene from Downton Abbey.
- ✓ Once, my friend and our "Queen of Visibility," Brandi Hand, and I were lunching in their Library Lounge during a business meeting. Our server was wearing a nametag that proclaimed her the employee of the month for July 2015. We asked her about it, and she humbly smiled. However, when we pressed her for details, she shared a story that had us in tears. Every afternoon the Inn at Biltmore serves a formal tea, much like one the Vanderbilts would have enjoyed in their heyday. She

regularly served a guest who came often to the tea. It was a favorite pastime for this lady. Sadly, the woman became terminally ill and was unable to return to the Inn. Our server took it upon herself to get approval from the senior leadership to bring the tea service to the woman's home—an amazing experience for all involved and a beautiful memory for the woman's family and friends. It's people like this Biltmore team member who remind us what *real* customer service is truly about—gestures of kindness that make people happy.

Above and Beyond

Mary Jo Pipkin, the executive director of Keystone Cedars and Keystone Place, a senior living community in Cedar Rapids, Iowa, made a "movie moment" when she decided the answer was yes, but the question was, "How?"

✓ A woman named Jan came to her very distressed. She was an only child, living in Iowa, while her parents lived in Cape Cod, Massachusetts. She desperately wanted her father to live closer to her but, understandably, her father wouldn't come unless her mother could come as well. Her mom was living in a nursing home on the Cape. Jan did not know how she could pull off moving her mother, who was in the advanced stages of dementia, to Iowa all by herself. It felt like an insurmountable challenge. She was on the verge of deciding to wait until her mom had passed. After brainstorming several options, Mary Jo offered this idea: What if two of the certified nursing assistants who worked at the assisted living community flew out to

Massachusetts with Jan and then flew back with her and her mother? That's just what they did.

✓ The caregivers were quite excited, as one had never been on a plane or seen the ocean before. They flew out to Massachusetts and enjoyed a lobster dinner with Jan and Bob, Jan's father, that evening. The next day, they flew back with Jan's mother, assisting her with restroom visits and connections, and keeping her calm during the flight. Bob moved to Keystone Place and his wife moved to a nearby skilled nursing center where her husband and daughter could visit her regularly.

These are the kind of creative, above-and-beyond decisions that inspire loyal customers and raving fans. Here are a few more gems:

✓ A housekeeper at a Methodist Senior Services community noticed that a particular resident, who had lived there for a while, had clothes that were starting to wear. She didn't have family to pay attention and bring in fresh clothes. As the person who washed, folded, and hung up her clothes on a daily basis, the housekeeper realized that the resident must not have someone on the outside to provide for her. She mentioned this to no one. Instead, she saved up money from her own paycheck, went to a thrift store, and purchased some very nice pieces of clothing. She took them home, washed and mended them, and presented them to the resident. The woman was so blown away and said she felt like she had gone on a shopping spree.

Jerod Guida, a Minneapolis-based realtor, amazes his clients with a commitment to do whatever it takes to help them achieve their goals. For example:

✓ When one of his clients, a motivated seller with very little furniture, couldn't afford a professional stager, Jerod moved in some of his own living room furniture in time for a scheduled showing. The house sold five days later and the client was delighted.

✓ One prospective client, who wasn't occupying the home he was trying to sell, hired a landscaping service to put down new sod. Jerod offered to watch the sprinklers over the weekend. Late Sunday night, during an extended period of drought, Jerod noticed one of the sprinklers had broken. He jumped in his car, ran to a local home store, and bought a new one. The clients were so impressed they gave Jerod the listing, which he sold in less than two weeks.

As we shall see, going above and beyond the call of duty doesn't only elicit wows from customers; it also results in sales.

Small Acts, Big Impact

✓ When staffers at the Tampa International Airport received a panicked call from the mother of 6-year-old Owen, who had left his beloved stuffed tiger, Hobbes, behind, they sprang into action. The crew found Hobbes and brought him to the Airport Operations Center, managed by Tony A'iuto. Because the family wouldn't be picking up Hobbes for a few more days, he saw the perfect opportunity to take some entertaining photos. He took Hobbes on a fun adventure around the airport and snapped photos along the way. When Owen and his family returned, they were treated to a photo book full of Hobbes's memories, such as meeting the air traffic controllers and the firefighters, riding in a luggage cart, and even working out at the airport gym! "Tony's got an interesting background," says Emily Nipps, the communications manager for Tampa International Airport. "He began his career in theme parks [and] went on to law enforcement, working as a dispatcher. Later he was a member of a hostage negotiation team before coming to work for us. So he's got a very caring heart combined with a sense of humor and a knack for having fun on the job." The story quickly went viral, sprinting through the national and international media. More importantly, Owen can feel secure knowing that Hobbes was just fine for the little bit of time they were apart!

Here's a similar story from Splendido of Mather LifeWays:

✓ When one couple moved into Splendido, a continuing care retirement community in Tucson, Arizona, they brought their dog, Pepper, along. Pepper was understandably antsy due to the move. So, to enable her owners to take care of their business without having to worry about their pooch, VP of sales Gale Morgan kept him in her office. Pepper sat at her feet for two hours while Gale worked.

✓ To ensure a special experience for both Pepper and his "pack," she took random photos throughout their time together. For the next week, she kept sending her new residents photos with notes that read, "Here's what Pepper did while you were busy!" or "Here's what Pepper did while you were out doing errands!"

✓ "At one point," laughs Gale, "Pepper was sitting on my lap while I worked on the computer. We even took a selfie and posted it to Facebook!"

Some of the best "movie moment" stories come from people in the audience when I'm speaking. Here are two terrific examples:

✓ A woman brought her car to be fixed by her local auto mechanic. Coming out of their CD player were the sounds of the O'Jays, one of her favorite singing groups from back in the day. Unable to help herself, she started dancing and singing along, exclaiming to her mechanic how much she loved that group. The next day, she returned to pick up her vehicle. Not only was her car fixed and cleaned, but when she turned the key in the ignition, the sounds of the O'Jays were coming out of her car stereo. Her mechanic had taken the time to burn a CD just for her.

✓ Another woman found it hard to find a clothing store she truly liked. One day, she wandered into a new store and fell in love—with the clothes, the service, and the prices. She was so excited that she wrote to the corporate office expressing her delight. Two weeks later, she arrived home to find a box on her porch. Upon opening it, she discovered it was filled with beautiful clothes in her size along with a note from the CEO of the company that read, "We're so glad you found our store! We hope you come back often and bring friends. In the meantime, here are some complimentary outfits for you to enjoy." You can bet she comes back often—with friends.

Here are some other small gestures that made a big impression:

✓ Charlie Flynn-McIver is the cofounder of North Carolina Stage Company, the professional equity theater in Asheville, North Carolina. When Charlie noticed that I was bringing my group "Ladies Who Love Live Theatre" to a performance that night, he sent me an e-mail asking where we were dining first. He popped into the restaurant to personally thank us for coming to his theater *and* invited us to take a backstage tour after the show.

✓ Upon learning that it was the hundredth meeting of "Ladies Who Love Live Theatre," Charlie and his wife and fellow cofounder, Angie, stopped by our restaurant again to thank us for our support. Susan Harper, the director of the Asheville Community Theatre, welcomed us personally in her curtain speech that evening, and gave every lady in attendance a coupon for a free drink. It's the fantastic performances *and* the personal touch that keep us attending shows at North Carolina Stage Company and Asheville Community Theatre over and over again.

✓ "Sometimes our *wow* stories are the little things cast members do that would not happen anywhere else," says Maggie Deering, HR manager for Hollywood Casino in Joliet, Illinois. "For example, a member of our environmental services team once cleaned gum off the bottom of a guest's shoe, all while she continued to play her slot machine, resulting in no interruption in her enjoyment of her game. We also had a couple with a seafood allergy come into our [crab leg] buffet...one night, which they could not enjoy. Our sous chef went out of his way to come to their table and find out what type of seafood, if any, they could eat. He proceeded to hand-deliver several seafood items they enjoyed.

✓ When Mike Calvin, of First Fruits Consulting, hired a company called Sourdough Transfer of Fairbanks, Alaska, to help him pack up some household items for a move, the word "hospitality" didn't immediately jump to mind. However, when the crew showed up 30 minutes early for a 9 a.m. job, he was impressed. After noticing him and his wife hanging around ready to help, the crew leader said, "You hired us so you could relax. So relax!" Mike was thrilled. When they completed the job with care and courtesy, he felt like they were old friends. Mike was so impressed, he wrote about them in a column entitled "Amazing Customer Service in Unexpected Situations" for Daily News Miner.

✓ A member of my team spoke to Karen Conover, the owner of Sourdough Transfer. Karen shared this story that shows that sometimes simple honesty can delight a customer. "One of our movers was in a bedroom packing up the lady's household goods when he came across a really large gold nugget. He took it to her and said, 'Ma'am, we don't pack [these kind of valuable items], so you might want to take this.' She was in tears because she had lost it and was so grateful he had the honesty and integrity to bring it to her. It's always such a big fear with people, because they are trusting us with their possessions. It was a normal day for us, but a *wow* moment for her!"

✓ NightGlass Media Group is a video production and Web-design company located in Duluth, Georgia, just north of Atlanta. When they wanted to thank a customer for the repeat business he was sending their way, they sent a mobile detailer to his establishment to clean his cars. "We were trying to think outside the box and not just send the typical *lunch on us*," explains Colleen Voisin, NightGlass's business development manager. "We didn't just focus on the executive cars, either. They were impressed, need-less to say, and we received many compliments from their staff." What a way to show gratitude and knock your cus-tomers' socks off at the same time!

✓ I always send bulk orders of my books over to *www.800CEORead.com* because they provide me and my customers with excellent service and great discount prices. However, it was a movie moment for me when the company sent me a completely unexpected box of free books with a thank-you note for giving them my business.

✓ As a dog lover, I can imagine the worry proud parents of pups must have when they check their dogs into the luggage compartment of airplanes. On a Delta airlines flight, I was impressed to see a pilot personally update a passenger on the status of his pet. "What a beautiful dog," he said. "I looked in on him just a minute ago, and he's settled in and doing just fine." I'm sure this information relieved the passenger and made the flight that much more comfortable for him. Sometimes, it's the "little" things that make the "movie moments."

Honoring the Fallen

With Delta's permission, I'm republishing this blog post found on Delta Airline's Website. It was written by Michael Thomas and posted on July 4, 2015:

> Earlier this year, as our plane pushed from gate A19 in Atlanta, I observed a man standing alone on the ramp. He was prominently holding the American flag, paying tribute as our aircraft slowly taxied by. Despite the hustle of ground vehicles and airplanes, time seemed to stand still as the flag gently waved in the breeze.
>
> Beneath our feet, a fallen hero in a flag-draped casket was being escorted home to his or her final resting place. Brian McConnell, the man who stood until our aircraft passed

out of sight, is a member of the Delta Honor Guard, which represents the airline as it helps carry home the remains of America's service women and men. I sat down with Brian; here's his story:

"For nearly a decade, I've stood alongside a dedicated group of Delta Air Lines volunteers, rain or shine, to pay respects to our nation's fallen heroes as they transit through the world's busiest airport. As a member of the Delta Honor Guard, we take great pride in the humbling task of making sure the remains of these military fallen are well cared for as they make their way home.

The ceremony is somber yet dignified as we pull the casket from the belly of the aircraft while displaying each flag from the five branches of the military behind the saluting hand of the fallen soldier's military escort. I recite a prayer while the remains are carefully secured in an awaiting, specially made cart before turning to the escort to present the escort with a Delta Honor Guard coin to be given to the fallen soldier's next of kin.

It's a sobering experience to stand in tribute while customers on board the airplane and in the terminal as well as the family and escort look on, but it's our way of serving our country and ensuring our heroes are well cared for on their journey home. The women and men of the employee-led Honor Guard, many of whom have served in the Armed Forces, have helped transport home more than 3,000 remains through Atlanta's airport. We've served soldiers of current conflicts as well as the repatriated remains of those from foreign conflicts in Korea, Vietnam, World War II, and others. We also provide honorable tribute to first responders, firefighters, and law enforcement. I'm proud and humbled knowing our Guard has grown to include other Delta markets including Minneapolis, Detroit, Salt Lake City, Los Angeles, and Washington, D.C.

I came from a family of servicemen. My father and uncles all served, and my eldest son today continues his active duty service in the United States Air Force. I have never had the honor of service, but this is my way of serving and my way of preserving the dignity and honor of those who have served."

Process for Preference

Hans Van Der Reijden, managing director of hotel operations and educational initiatives at The Hotel at Auburn University, is a wealth of information when it comes to giving individualized service and delighting guests.

✓ He suggests we cultivate our powers of observation to determine preferences. "We try to figure out the purpose of our guests' visits. Are they a on a business trip? Here for a family vacation? Or is it a special occasion? A business traveler coming to the front desk and dropping his bag or pulling out his credit card does not want to discuss his drive, the weather, or his hometown. He wants to be checked in as fast and efficiently as he can by someone with an incredible smile and an offer to do whatever we can for him while he's here. If you have a family of four pull up wearing flip flops, shorts, and sunglasses, you take a different approach. You want to take them to the pool and show them the restaurant. In a restaurant, if a couple is gazing into each other's eyes and holding hands, you don't want to check in every five seconds to see how they like the meal. You want to be as unobtrusive as you possibly can. If you're cleaning a room and there are four empty

Diet Dr. Pepper cans in the trash, take note. That's a preference. If we observe this, and put a note of it in our system, the guest will get it next time without even asking."

✓ To that end, his staff is armed with tiny little "preference pads" that become part of their uniform. Whether it's a front desk associate, a housekeeper, or a banquet server, they are tasked with observing the preferences of guests, noting it on their pads, and making sure it goes into their system. "Engineers walk around with them, too. Nobody gets more time with a guest than an engineer in the room if something is not working. You're in somebody's private space for about 20 minutes and you learn a lot. At the end of the day, the purpose for us to be here is not to fulfill a task or function, but to take care of our customers. If you really get that, then you're going to find a lot of joy in learning about the guests and giving them little surprises."

✓ Here's an example of that culture of observation in action at The Hotel at Auburn University: "We are connected to Auburn University in many ways, and one of them is through the vet school program here in Auburn. It's one of the top three in the country, and people literally fly from all over to have their pets treated here," says Hans. "We are a pet-friendly hotel. People stay here for weeks at a time while their dog or cat is going through chemo or whatever. You can just see it when someone is dealing with a sick child or pet. It affects you emotionally. A group of front desk employees got together to see what they could do to personalize a stay for [these pets], especially for when someone is here a longer time." They now provide personalized mats, bowls in the Auburn University colors, and Milk Bones with orange and blue ribbons around them.

✓ The hotel, like any, has its regular guests. Two of them were a couple known as "Mr. and Mrs. Merry Christmas," due to the Christmas tree farms they owned all over the southeast. They came on the weekends for every home football game, for 26 years, until their health no longer allowed it. Everyone loved them. "So, one day I get this phone call," says Hans, "asking me to come to the lobby and speak to a guest. In hotel lingo, that means someone is yelling, kicking, and demanding to see the general manager. So you walk into the lobby waving a white flag and you just try to listen and figure out what to do for the customer. In this case, I see Mr. Merry Christmas, an 85-year-old man, crying in the lobby. I'm thinking, *Oh my goodness! What did we do to him and why?*"

✓ At his invitation, Hans followed Mr. Merry Christmas to his room. There was his wife sitting there with three front desk agents wearing Santa hats and Christmas caroling in September, next to a little tree complete with lights and gifts. "This is the greatest thing anybody has ever done for us!" exclaimed Mr. Merry Christmas.

As you can see, it doesn't take a lot to make a "movie moment." It merely takes observation, creativity, and, maybe, a Santa hat or two.

✓ When Pam Huff was the director of celebrity services at the Gaylord Opryland Hotel, she was no stranger to making "movie moments" for her VIP guests. Each guest under her team's jurisdiction was provided with personalized amenities and treated to many unexpected moments throughout their stay. Pam would encourage her team not to give guests all their treats at once, but to spread them out. She wanted her team to wow them upon their arrival, but hold a few surprises back so they were continually delighted throughout their stay.

✓ Begin keeping a "favorites list" for your customers or greatest referral sources. What are their favorite foods? Restaurants? Hobbies? Sports teams? What's their alma mater? What kind of music do they love? The more you know about your customers, the more prepared you are to make a movie moment.

Oprah Moments

These are the once-in-a-lifetime, dream-come-true, did-that-really-just-happen moments that get you thinking that Oprah must be around somewhere. The following illustrative story was shared by professional speaker and entertainer (and my good friend) David Glickman:

My family was visiting the Hard Rock Café at Universal Studios in Orlando a few years ago. For those who don't know, Hard Rock Café is famous for having lots of rock-and-roll memorabilia throughout its restaurants. The booth where my wife and I and our two sons were seated had an amazing piece of memorabilia on the wall above us. It was an original cornet [like a trumpet] that was played on the Beatles' "All You Need Is Love" and "Penny Lane." There was also a page from the original score of a Beatles orchestration signed by all four Beatles. For a huge Beatles fan like myself, this was nirvana. It was a great meal and a great experience.

Flash-forward a year. We're back at Universal Studios. (We live in Tampa, so it's less than a two-hour drive.) We decide to go back to Hard Rock Café for lunch. We specifically ask for that booth because I wanted to sit again underneath the cornet that played those iconic horn lines in those two iconic Beatles songs. After a little bit of juggling parties, we were able to be seated in that booth again—and, again, a great meal and a great experience.

On the way out, we stopped by the hostess's stand, and I thanked the hostess for helping us to sit in my favorite booth. She leaned forward and in an almost-whisper asked me, "Are you a big Beatles fan?" I said, "Yes I am!" She leaned in even closer and asked, "Have you ever seen the Lennon Room?" I said, 'No! I don't even know what that is." She said, "Would you like to see the Lennon Room?" And I said, "Well, yes. That sounds great"—still not knowing what it was. She said, "Just wait here. I'll get someone to show it to you."

Within three minutes, a young man approached us and said, "So you want to see the Lennon Room?" And I said, "Yes, we most certainly do. Oh, and by the way, what *is* the Lennon Room?" He laughed and said, "Come on, I'll show you." He then proceeded to give the four of us a private, behind-the-scenes tour of the Hard Rock Café at Universal which, we came to learn, is among many other things the world's largest Hard Rock Café. We saw a warehouse-sized storage area that housed many miscellaneous items that were not on display in the restaurant, including such amazing items as one of the bicycles ridden by the Beatles in the movie *Help!* He allowed us to take photos galore and take as much time as we wanted.

The tour ended in the Lennon Room, which was an exact replica of the living room of John Lennon's apartment at the Dakota in New York. Actual furniture from the apartment, donated by Yoko Ono, was in the room, along with other memorabilia that was jaw-dropping in its significance in rock-and-roll history. We had been on this private tour for almost an hour and I found myself getting teary-eyed at what I was experiencing. And how it all came about because the hostess picked up on my Beatles interest and asked, "Are you a big Beatles fan?" I have to think that employees are taught to look for opportunities like this to "surprise and amaze" the guest. It was one of the greatest customer service experiences I have ever had.

✓ United Parcel Service (UPS) launched a program called "Your Wishes Delivered" in November 2014. Customers were asked to tweet their wishes using the hashtag #WishesDelivered. For each wish posted to Facebook or Twitter, UPS donates a dollar to one of three charity partners. A few wishes are chosen and granted.

✓ One example is 4-year-old Carson in Denver, Colorado. UPS Driver Ernie Lagasca has been delivering packages to Carson's home since the boy was an infant. Carson loves trucks. He and "Mr. Ernie" have developed a special relationship. (Carson even wants to grow up to be a UPS driver!) The team at UPS decided to grant Carson's wish sooner rather than later. They sent Mr. Ernie to Carson's neighborhood with a special delivery. Carson was delighted to find that inside the big UPS truck was a mini, battery-powered truck just for him. He and his special friend spent the afternoon delivering packages and smiles throughout his neighborhood.

Birthdays and Holidays

Birthdays and holidays present an easy opportunity to create special movie moments for your customers year-round. Here are some examples:

✓ Rather than sending a commercial birthday card, Rick Salmeron delivers his birthday wishes by recording a short video and sending it to each client.

✓ Shanna Henkel, owner of The Village Coffee Shop in Boulder, Colorado, writes the birthdays of regular customers on a calendar. When they come in on or around their special day, they are often surprised when she wishes them a happy birthday and treats them to a birthday breakfast.

✓ I recently attended something called Keynote Camp, which was led by storyteller and humorous motivational speaker Kelly Swanson, and hosted by the equally hilarious professional speaker Laurie Guest, owner of Solutions are Brewing. This is an amazing three-day experience, created by Kelly, where professional speakers can practice their craft and take their speeches up to a whole new level. (Incidentally, Laurie has a red-carpet program of her own. No surprise she was the hostess-with-the-mostest, and the camp experience was amazing!) In the middle of a session, I noticed a Facebook message alerting me that it was Kelly's birthday. She, of course, had not told a soul. I quietly mentioned it to Laurie, who sprung into action. Within a few hours, Laurie had not only videotaped each of us sharing a special birthday wish for Kelly, but e-mailed several of the birthday girl's closest friends to send in their video clips from around the country, as well. "The coolest part," exclaims Laurie, "is that everyone responded within the hour!" No surprise, really. It makes people feel good to do good things for the people they care about. Laurie was able to edit it all together and show it to Kelly that evening. The birthday girl proclaimed it "the nicest thing anyone had ever done for [her] birthday!"

✓ One of my former bosses used to give every employee a "Birthday in a Bag" on our special days. It was a paper grocery bag with a cake (that he baked himself!), candles, two party hats, two party plates, two cups, and napkins. It was all tied together with a big balloon. People wondered where he found the time. He definitely had a loyal group of team members thanks to these little gestures of thoughtfulness.

✓ Most of us have had that feeling of dread upon hearing the sirens and seeing those flashing blue lights in our rearview mirror, knowing that we were about to be pulled over by the police. Imagine how quickly your dread would turn to relief and glee if, instead of writing you a ticket, the officer handed you presents! This example of holiday spirit was demonstrated by the police department of Lowell, Michigan, during their #upliftsomeone campaign. Officers pulled people over under the pretense of citing them for a minor traffic violation. During the 15 minutes or so the officer was with the driver, he or she would ask seemingly random questions to discover what was on the driver's holiday shopping list. Other Lowell Police Department staffers were at a nearby store listening in on radios, quickly purchasing the gifts, and getting them to the pull-over spot in time for the officer to surprise the motorist. The surprise was the brainchild of Rob Bliss of Rob Bliss Creative, and the chief of police, Steve Bukala. It was sponsored by UP TV in Atlanta. "The response," says the Chief, "was off the scale!" The video went viral and had more than 35 million views in less than a week. However, even more exciting were the reactions of the recipients. "There was one dad who had lost his job. Mom was starting a new job, but money was tight. He told me, 'I'll bring them back if I have to,'" relates Chief Bukala. "I said, 'No, these are yours to keep.' The man was beside himself. It was what he wanted to get for his children but couldn't afford." Officer Scott, the policeman who was pulling over the lucky citizens, was reluctant to participate at first. However, he ended up loving it. "He'll tell you it was the best day of his career!" says the chief. Now there's the ticket to positive police/ citizen relations!

Here are a few more perhaps less-dramatic ways to surprise and delight clients and customers:

✓ Darlene Tenes, owner of Casa Q, spends one day at the end of the year baking homemade cookies for her best clients. She sends them in beautiful boxes.

✓ For shopping centers the December holidays are often the busiest season. For Westfield Shopping Centers, it is no different. Millions of guests stop in to fulfill their shopping needs, visit with Santa, or just gather with friends and family as they enjoy the season. Jeff Adams, senior director of customer service and marketing, says, "For many years, our service culture at Westfield has been about finding opportunities to exceed the expectations of our guests, own every interaction, and win over the hearts of everyone who comes through our doors. As part of our overall holiday strategy [in 2013], we wanted to find a way to bring service even more to the forefront during our busiest time of year." Enter the Westfield Merry Makers.

✓ "We're here to make your holidays happier," says Jeff. "We wanted to make the holiday shopping period a little less stressful and a *lot* more fun by creating unexpected moments of surprise and delight and performing random acts of kindness." The Westfield Merry Makers played three primary roles at Westfield centers: They provided random performances, random acts of kindness, and random gifts.

- Random performances included mini flash mobs, caroling throughout the center, surprising guests with the mistletoe stick, and keeping them in shape after all those sweet treats with "Elf-ercise," in which they were encouraged to "prance like a reindeer."

- Random acts of kindness included greeting guests at entrances with candy canes, carrying packages to guests' cars, carrying food trays for guests in the dining terrace, shuttling guests to their cars in the cold weather, and complimentary gift wrapping.

- Random gifts from Westfield and the Merry Makers added to the surprise and delight, and included everything from the basics of chocolates, bottled water, hot cocoa, and shopping totes, to the over-the-top moments of treating a family to dinner with VIP reservations at top restaurants, walking into coffee shops and paying for their orders, and presenting Westfield gift cards.

"In addition to providing excellence in service, we wanted to allow people to tell stories about us and motivate them to return and shop more," adds Jeff. It worked. The program was extremely well-received. Guests began telling their friends and asking for a schedule so they could be sure to return to experience the Merry Makers in person. The program was brought back by popular demand in 2014 for another successful year of surprise-and-delight moments.

✓ Speaking of the holiday season, the WestJet Christmas miracle program is another example of a making "movie moments." The company chooses a flight and, using a real-time video of Santa, collects the Christmas wishes of passengers prior to boarding. The unsuspecting people sit through the flight and head over to baggage claim upon landing, expecting to see their luggage. Unbeknownst to them, WestJet employees, who are based at the passengers' destination, have been frantically shopping and wrapping gifts. Instead of suitcases, beautifully wrapped and tagged presents come down the beltway. The astonishment and celebration of the recipients was captured on video and significantly increased brand awareness of the airline through distribution on social media. More importantly, what fun for both the WestJet team members and their customers!

✓ "The WestJet holiday video may have gotten the most attention, but it's not the only one," says Robert Palmer, manager of public relations. Yet another heartwarming experience centered on a father whose child was in the hospital. "We do a lot of work with national charitable partners like Ronald McDonald house, which houses families when they have to stay in a city that isn't their home because they have a child in the hospital. When your child is very sick, as parents, you have to split up. One has to stay at the hospital, hotel, or nearest Ronald McDonald house. Eventually, one of you has to go home and make money to sustain the family. This happens to families all over North America every day." In one notable example, a WestJet employee actually trained for one father's day job (cleaning transit buses for a city in Western Canada) and was then able to replace the man for a week while he stayed with his sick child, who needed a heart transplant. WestJet then flew the father out for Father's Day and a week-long visit with his family. He spent time with his loved ones while the WestJet employee spent the week doing his job for him. "Creating these experiences for people is rooted in our culture of care," says Robert. "That's what it's all about. We videotape them to share them with people who can't witness it firsthand." The video was updated after the little boy received his heart—arguably the best gift of all.

Red Carpet Resources

✓ A great resource for literally rolling out the red carpet for your customers is *www.redcarpets.com*. You can purchase an actual red carpet, complete with its own bag, a background with your logo on it, and even stanchions and velvet ropes. In fact, you can order carpet runways in a variety of colors. When I wanted to wow the team at Mather LifeWays, I sent them a carpet in their company color, orange.

✓ Giving your corporate clients anything with their company logo on it is a sure way to make a movie moment. One resource for these personalized sweet treats is WickedGoodCookies.com, based in my childhood home of Massachusetts.

✓ If you'd like to contact Hollywood stars directly to give your customers a taste of the real red carpet, a great resource is *www.contactanycelebrity.com*. It is the most up-to-date database for celebrity contact information.

A Very Personal Movie Moment

My beloved father, Philip Bouchard, passed away in May 2012. He was loving, fun, funny, and passionate about his family. My sister and I were blessed to call him Dad. One of the things I learned from him was his work ethic. He was not only dedicated to doing his best at whatever job was in front of him, but he did it with a smile. People gravitated toward him because of his good humor and amazing attitude.

Before he died, he worked as an assistant produce manager for Publix supermarkets. At one time, had owned his own delicatessen and small neighborhood store in Fall River, Massachusetts, which he called, to everyone's amusement, Phil-a-Deli. However, for most of my childhood, Dad was a construction worker and foreman.

A couple of years after my dad was gone, my mom was going through some items and found this letter, presumably written by a tenant in one of the apartment buildings he worked on:

To whom it may concern:

This is to say thanks to one of the bosses with your company for his understanding and kindness in a bad situation this morning. His first name is Philip and he is probably Irish or Italian due to his medium complexion. [My Dad was actually French. Close?]

My pet cat, Martha, was stuck under the new bathtub when the men arrived to work in the bathroom. Nothing worked to get her out. The men banged and pounded and kicked but it served only to make her more frightened. They were going to close the wall around the tub today. I was almost freaked out with horror. They said the tub could not be moved. It was rooted.

This nice man came in and asked me how everything was. I told him about Martha. He quietly went into the bathroom and, without a word, lifted up the bathtub. With that, Martha ran out and under the chair where I could get her and put her in the bedroom.

The other men were nice but I believe they would have gone ahead anyway. I love Martha and have had her for years. She would not have wanted to die.

Can you imagine me taking a bath with my cat dying under the tub?

It may be only a minor thing to you, sir. But to me, it showed someone very special is around. He has an unusual way about him anyway, being polite, kind, and understanding. When everyone else is rushing around making a racket, this man brings a quiet moment.

So, he spoke well of your company through that act of kindness. I shall repeat it and mention your company, as well.

Shirley

South Boston, MA

Sometimes, you make a "movie moment" simply by doing the right thing. Thanks for the reminder, Dad.

Questions for Discussion

- What's our process for preference?
- Do our team members have what they need to make movie moments for our customers?
- Which idea will we implement first?

CHAPTER FIVE

Cut! Take Two!

When you're committed to delivering a red-carpet experience, you must always strive for flawless service. Even with the best of intentions, however, we sometimes make mistakes and have to face unhappy customers. Let's be honest: sometimes they are unhappy even when we *didn't* make a mistake! Either way, how you recover in those moments can make the difference between an angry, loose-cannon customer and a raving fan!

According to a study done by the Research Industry of America, anywhere from 54 to 70 percent of complaining customers will continue to do business with you *if* they receive a response to their criticism. If they feel their grievance was resolved, that number goes up to 95 percent.

Emily Loeks, the director of community affairs for Celebration! Cinema, knows this. That's why the theatre chain once employed a "director of Hollywood endings" to respond to unhappy guests. She tells this story to illustrate:

> One time a customer wrote a comment card asking if we had
> changed the way we cooked our pretzels at one of our theaters.
> In reality, we hadn't. Our pretzels were being prepared the

same way they had for the last two or three years. Initially, she got a fairly straight-forward reply that the recipe was the same. She gave us a pretty frustrated response, stating that she was quite sure and that her recent experience with a pretzel in our cinema was not what she had come to expect! This was one of our really great customers. So, I'm sure we would have happily given her a refund. Then we realized that what she really wanted was a good pretzel. This particular cinema was adjacent to a mall that had an Auntie Anne's Pretzel. So, we got her a gift certificate for Auntie Anne's. Then we went into Meijer (our local store) and purchased about four to five high-quality varieties of pretzels, including chocolate covered ones, and sent her a gift basket full of those items and a note of appreciation. She called almost in tears because she felt like she'd had a bad moment and got a bit overzealous. Maybe she had just had a bad pretzel. Yet the fact that someone responded so creatively with concern for her as a customer of our business was really meaningful, and she was so appreciative. Those are the kind of moments that we like to create with our customers. We strive to ensure that people know that we take it seriously and that the small stuff matters.

What a great story, and what a wonderful example of how a challenging situation with an unhappy customer can still have, well, a Hollywood ending.

✓ The team at Celebration! Cinema uses the acronym THEATRE to remember how to assist a less-than-happy customer:

☐ Thank the customer. (Making that the first response de-escalates the situation and enables you to have a more constructive exchange.)

- ☐ **H**ear and acknowledge. (Really listen and reflect back what the customer is saying.)
- ☐ **E**mpathize with the customer. (Regardless of whether or not you agree with them, empathize with your customers. We are all human.)
- ☐ **A**pologize with sincerity.
- ☐ **T**ake care of the problem. (If it can be fixed quickly, do so. If it's more of a culture problem, take the next step.)
- ☐ The next step is **R**eport it. (If the same issue is coming up two or three times, you know you need to dig into this a little more to find a permanent solution.)
- ☐ Go the **E**xtra mile. (Find a way to go the extra mile for the guest.)

Acronyms and models like this can help your team members understand exactly what to do when faced with a complaining customer.

This is the shortest chapter in this book. As you can imagine, it's not easy for people to share their mistakes with others. Trust me, we all make them, and we all have challenges with a few less-than-happy customers, whether we actually made the mistake or not. So, as short as this chapter is, it's an important one. I'm hoping the ideas, examples, and advice of the few who did share will help you know what to do when you find it's time to say, "Cut! Take two!"

What Can I Do to Make it Right?

This advice comes from Hans Van Der Reijden, of The Hotel at Auburn University:

- ✓ "When it comes to service recovery, you must empower your employees to handle any issue that is brought to their attention by a customer," says Hans. "If the first thing they do is deflect by asking a manager or supervisor, or offering the guest the opportunity to talk to a manager, you've just ignited the customer."

This is so important at The Hotel at Auburn University that the first two hours of orientation are all about that. Relates Hans, "I always ask the question, 'Have you ever been to a restaurant where something was overcooked or undercooked, or took too long, or whatever the case may be?' And you bring it to the attention of your server who says, '*Let me get my manager*'? In all the years I've been asking that question in orientation, I have never once found a person who says they really like it when that happens." In Hans's opinion, 100 percent of people who are agitated and upset tell you so because they are hoping *you* will take care of it—not so you can foist the problem onto someone else. "Then, [customers] have to explain their case all over again and they just get angrier. This is not what you want."

The solution, according to Hans, is to *empower* your employees to handle any situation that comes their way. Train them, then trust them. When I asked Hans whether this meant that employees were given a certain dollar amount to work with, he replied immediately. "Absolutely not! I strongly disagree with that. What you [would be] saying to them is that you trust them only up to $100. You can't do that."

"So, you're saying they can make any decision whatsoever to satisfy the guest?" I asked.

"Yes," Hans replied. "Otherwise, you're not truly empowering them. Once every two weeks, I teach a two-hour class on that to our new employees. It is really to make one thing abundantly clear: You are empowered. This," he stresses, "is really important."

✓ Hans's research has also indicated that although we often tend to think the majority of people complain because they want something for free, in most cases this is not true. "They are throwing you a lifeline because they like you and they know you can't allow this to happen. The moment you start throwing free stuff at them, you've made the situation much worse."

So, what is a customer-service superstar to do? You ask this magic question: "What can I do to make it right?"

Then you actually act on the answer!

Giving us the perfect example of what can happen when employees are empowered to make it right, Ed Eynon shares this story of service recovery, which took place at the Hotel del Coronado, one of the KSL Resort Properties:

In the company's "4 Keys to Creating Guests for Life" hospitality service training, we strive to answer the question "Which element of service is the most important—the technical component or the hospitality component?" In an effort to do this, our training manager at the Hotel del Coronado, Patrick Masters, uses an example of guest feedback received through our Unifocus customer survey. The example he uses is from the housekeeping section of this particular survey:

"Our room was exceptional! Our beds were turned down each night and we loved the extra touch of placing a sea shell on the bed. We had a problem with our refrigerator overheating and it was fixed promptly. There was a break in the hot water pipe that affected our room during one of the nights, and we were notified by a letter placed under our door explaining the problem. The pipe was fixed on time and we had hot water again in the morning. We couldn't ask for better service."

[Patrick] reads the example and leads a discussion regarding the missing/damaged technical components and the impact that could have on the guests' perception and enjoyment. He then refers to the overall Unifocus score, which was 100 [a perfect score]. The question asked is: "What do you think remedied the two glaringly obvious technical missteps (no hot water and broken mini-fridge)?" The answer is the hospitality component of service, which consequently happens to be the most important component, as well.

The remainder of the review also highlights other examples of the service this couple received. Among these, the couple, who were celebrating their 30th wedding anniversary, were offered a free room upgrade, had their boarding passes printed by the concierge, and were wished a happy anniversary by many of the Hotel del Coronado associates.

In the Overall Stay notes at the end of the survey, the couple writes:

"We travel relatively infrequently, but our visit to San Diego and in particular, our stay at the Hotel del Coronado to celebrate our 30th wedding anniversary, made lasting memories for both my wife Sherry and me. We definitely intend to return again in the future. We're so glad that we chose the Hotel del Coronado to celebrate a milestone in our lives."

✓ It was the empowerment the team had to take care of the technical issues immediately, and the focus on hospitality using their four keys—warmth, personalization, awareness, and proactivity—that ensured a 100 rating despite a few missteps.

Take a Bow!

Equally important is the way you respond to employees when they make a mistake or have a mishap. You want to give your team members the sense that you're all in this together, and that, though you are absolutely going to do what's right for the customer at the same time, you have each other's backs.

Spencer Forgey, general manager of Mama D's Italian Kitchen, recalls this incident from his past:

When I was 19 and I was working at this upscale Chinese food restaurant up in L.A., we had to carry these big trays, with a big bowl of soup and then a bunch of small cups of soup out to a table and serve everyone at the table. I had an eight top [meaning eight people at a table]. They were a bunch of businesspeople. I was new and nervous. So I carried the tray out and set it down on a tray stand. As I'm serving the soup, the tray is uneven with weight and it falls. Bowls break and soup splatters everywhere! My manager comes out to me, just drops her head and shakes it disapprovingly. I was so scared I was going to lose my job.

That was my first time working in a restaurant and that was my experience. So, when I was hired on as a manager, I had that same reaction when something happened. The problem was that, in addition to the employee's embarrassment, every guest also felt some degree of the negative energy I was putting out there.

✓ Now, Spencer has a different reaction. Recently he watched one of the servers at Mama D's trip and drop a tray full of glasses. Every customer in the sold-out room stopped and looked. Instead of shaking his head or shaming the server, Spencer immediately announced, "Woo-hoo! Thank you! Thank you, everyone. She does all her own stunts!" That kind of humorous yet kind response ensures the energy stays positive and everyone stays happy.

✓ Another tip Spencer shares is the philosophy of "no mistakes, only lessons." In the previous example, the server was a little shaken up and lamented, "I made a mistake and everyone saw it."

Spencer asker her, "Did you get a lesson out of it?"

She replied. "Yeah, I'm not going to take that many glasses on one tray and I'm going to practice carrying it some more."

Perfect. That's a win-win. Spencer didn't even have to train her on the steps to prevent that kind of accident next time. She had the experience and learned firsthand what she should do. "Then, just like that," says Spencer, "the energy shifted. The rest of the night, everything was great!"

Turn it Around

If you read my previous book, *The Celebrity Experience*, you may recall the example of HUB Plumbing and Mechanical out of Boston, Massachusetts, whose team literally rolled out red carpets for their customers. John Wood, CEO, has since taken his company to New York City and changed many of his practices to meet the demand and style of his new market. Still, he is the number-one plumbing company on Yelp in his market. In New York that is no small feat! Does that mean he only gets five-star ratings? Nope. It's the way he addresses the negative reviews that turns them positive.

✓ John relates, "The funny thing is that, of course, I get one-star Yelp reviews from irate customers. With the exception of one review, I was able to call them and save it in some way. Typically, they are complaining over a small charge or a plumber who didn't communicate properly. The fact that I call them immediately disarms them, and once they realize I'm trying to repair the situation and make them happy, they typically calm right down."

John tries to narrow the situation down by finding out whether it was a matter of price, performance, or punctuality. "If it's a performance issue, I have the opportunity to meet with one of my plumbers and correct whatever went wrong. A lot of times, the guy was just having an off-day. If I can take a call that would have been a one-star review, go out on a Saturday to help him fix it, it can turn the whole thing around. So that's how I'm differentiating myself in what is arguably the most ferocious work environment on earth: New York."

John shakes his head at other service providers who waste time arguing over $300, regardless of who is right. He once gave back $1,200 to a customer. He was upset about it, but bit his tongue and gave it back. Six months later he got a call from that same customer who gave him a $65,000 job. "So, is that going to happen on every $1,200 you give back? Absolutely not! However, would it have happened on this one if I hadn't? Absolutely not!" This particular customer has since gone on and given John even more business. "If you go out of your way to make a customer happy," says John, "they'll typically do something nice in return."

Follow Up

Kendra Neal, director of client happiness at Ruby Receptionists, has a practice that creates a great impression even *after* the problem has been solved:

✓ "I think one of the biggest ways we create that red-carpet experience is the follow-up call. If something goes wrong or we make a big change to an account, or if we just think it will make an impact, we set a reminder for one to two weeks after the initial contact, call the client proactively, and ask: *How are things going? You and I talked a couple of weeks ago, and I wanted to make sure the error hasn't reoccurred and that the changes we made were exactly what you wanted.*" According to Kendra, what has become a normal practice at Ruby makes a huge impact on the client. She often hears astonished comments such as, "I can't believe you're following up with me personally! Who does that?"

When was the last time you called your phone provider or bank with a concern and they called you a week later just to make sure you were happy? When was the last time *you* did that for a customer?

✓ The other reminder Kendra provides is this: "Even when there's nothing you can do, there's always *something* you can do." Make it a challenge to turn unhappy customers into happy customers and you might just have fun doing it.

Go Out of Your Way

✓ Maggie Deering, from Penn National Gaming's Hollywood Casino in Joliet, offers this bit of advice: "Recovering with style means doing whatever it takes to get the customer what he or she needs." One time a regular casino guest went to the deli looking forward to his favorite roast beef sandwich. However, the deli was out of roast beef. Seeing his disappointment, a cast member (employee) took it upon herself to go to one of their other food outlets and have a sandwich created for him. She also brought a piece of his favorite lemon cake, on the house, to show appreciation for his business.

Social Media Savvy

As you can imagine, students at High Point University will often take to Twitter, Facebook, and other social media outlets to vent their frustration about, well, anything. They are often surprised, though, when Hillary Kokajko, senior director of interactive media, or Lyndsey Derrow, chief concierge, or one of their team picks up the phone to call them.

✓ "We respond to everything we see, but we rarely respond online. Why feed the beast? Instead, we personally reach out, face-to-face or by phone, to see what we can do to help. We resolve what we can. Nine times out 10, the post is erased by the student."

TREAT Your Upset Customers to Red-Carpet Customer Service

A model we've used at Red-Carpet Learning Systems that seems to have helped some of our clients is the idea of TREAT-ing upset customers to red-carpet service:

✓ Tune in and listen.
✓ Respond with empathy and regret.
✓ Explore solutions and fix the issue.
✓ Add the And Then Some (but not until you've done the above).
✓ Thank the customer.

Then, you want to ensure that the problem doesn't recur by discussing permanent fixes with your team. If customers are always complaining about the same issues and you're putting out the same fires, then you're just causing yourselves—and your customers—unnecessary heartache. It's important to put a process into place to listen effectively and respond to feedback, and come up with long-term solutions to prevent further problems. To do so you'll need:

✓ One or more ways to collect regular feedback from your customers.
✓ A commitment to regular review of that feedback with your team.

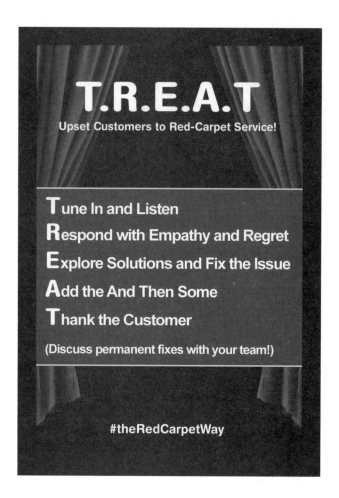

- ✓ A method for sorting, organizing, and prioritizing.
- ✓ A flagging system that predicts potential problems before they arise.
- ✓ A set of measurable goals to share with your team.
- ✓ A process for determining the root cause of any ongoing issues.
- ✓ An action plan for improvement.
- ✓ One simple method our clients use for continuous improvement that has worked really well was taught to me by

Pam Huff, former director of celebrity services for the Gaylord Opryland Hotel in Nashville, Tennessee. They are called "hit-or-miss reports." In essence, after each customer interaction you gather the involved team and evaluate how it went. What were your hits? (What did you do well?) What were your misses? (What could stand to be improved?) What will you do next time to ensure your misses turn into hits?

One of our clients, a head chef at a luxury senior living retirement community, used them with his team after every private party they gave for a resident. "At first," he said, "it felt like busy work. However, we soon saw that by discussing it and refining our process, what had been a long list of misses turned into a long list of hits." Better yet, more and more people began to request private parties as a result of their efforts. This was great because it was a profit center for the community. This means this process turned into positive bottom-line results.

Categorize the Situation

✓ Nina Swann, the front of the house coordinator for North Carolina Stage Company in Asheville, North Carolina, knows that when she receives a phone call from an upset patron, she must immediately consider which category applies to the situation.

1. The customer just needs to vent, in which case Nina listens and figures out a solution with them.
2. There was a misunderstanding, in which case the problem is solved with a calm, friendly explanation.
3. She won't be able to make them happy because they'd prefer to speak to someone at a higher level.

Says Nina, "Once I place the situation into the right category, we can find a solution rather quickly. Our goal is to always end a call with a happy customer. I have my front-of-house staff trained on the same basics and, thus far, it has been working well. It's all about communication and taking the time to find the real problem."

Use Your Experience for Good

One of my favorite examples of the power of red-carpet service recovery comes from High Point University. Roger Clodfelter is now the senior vice president of communications for HPU. However, when I first met him he was the director of WOW! Part of his job was to hand-deliver birthday cards for students on their birthday. The university was becoming known for such gestures. However, one day he received a call from a very upset mother claiming that he had forgotten her daughter's birthday.

✓ Of course, Roger immediately apologized and made restitution. The next thing he did was work to figure out and resolve the glitch in the system that caused the mistake to be made. But it's the final step he took that demonstrates the commitment to extraordinary service that produces red-carpet results. For many years, Roger shared the story of his own error with others to demonstrate the level of excellence expected at High Point University.

Do a Little Extra

✓ MyCorporation.com provides online document filing services for clients who wish to become a corporation or limited liability company. The company often offers to feature their clients on the company blog to give them some exposure. This is especially helpful as a little extra after employees have addressed a customer complaint. Says CEO Deborah Sweeney, "By giving free publicity to the customer and eradicating any problems they faced in their services, we are able to turn a dire situation into a full-fledged success. It is often not enough to simply fix the problem; you need to go above and beyond to create a new raving fan of the company."

Do Whatever it Takes

✓ L-Soft is an international tech company known for its e-mail program, LISTSERV. This story, shared by founder and CEO Eric Thomas, demonstrates how sometimes absorbing the cost of fixing a problem for a customer can come back to you tenfold:

> One morning, I received an urgent call from our support manager. The VP of a large Wall Street firm was on the phone, demanding to talk with the CEO. I knew only too well what this was about. For months, we had been trying to figure out why our software crashed about once a week for this customer. It was very frustrating for us, because they could only provide minimal information about the crashes due to the nature of the business. We had spent over 100 hours on the problem to no avail. No other customer we had was experiencing this problem.
>
> I remember taking the call in my kitchen, because it was the quietest room in the apartment. The VP complained that they had lost money, we had obviously been negligent, and that he wanted me to give him one reason not to transfer this to the legal department. I

suggested running the software on Windows while we worked on the problem, but he insisted he needed a solution within 48 hours, and procurement would take weeks. So I told him that as soon as I hung up, I would call our consultant department and have them pre-load and configure the software on a server, my treat. We should be able to make the next day deadline and they would have a solution within 24 to 48 hours.

Upon hearing that, the VP ended the call to give us as much time as possible to meet the deadline. We did. A few months later, they made a large purchase that more than made up for the cost of the server. The customer explained that the VP had been impressed at how far we had been willing to go to find a solution for them in spite of the very aggressive deadline and the fact that, at the time, they were not a very big customer.

Even When It's Their Fault

✓ Publix Supermarkets is known for its policy of replacing items for customers, no questions asked. My father, who once worked as the assistant produce manager for a Publix in Florida, told me the story of a woman who came in with her husband and headed to the butcher counter, asking to have her steaks replaced because they were bad. Her husband stood sheepishly behind her and said, "Go ahead. Tell them why they were bad." She replied, "I overcooked them." The butcher smiled and promptly gave her new steaks. Yes, sometimes a customer or two will take advantage of your policy—but most won't, and it's this practice that keeps customers raving about Publix's customer service.

Make Sure They Leave Happy

✓ Brian Meissner is the owner of a boutique hostel in a very remote area of Urguay called El Diablo Tranquilo. He knows that the sooner you gain customer feedback, the more likely you can turn a negative situation into a positive one. Says Brian, "Better customer service recovery was the driving force behind the development of our own Wi-Fi management system. We now require guests who have been on the property for at least 48 hours to rate their experience in order to continue using the Internet. The feedback is immediately emailed to our manager on duty. This means that whenever we're failing to meet expectations, our manager knows right away, while there is still time to rectify the situation. All too often," points out Brian, "disappointed customers prefer to avoid conflict with a staff member, and a problem goes unnoticed until a scathing Trip Advisor review appears weeks later. Now, with the satisfaction app we use as part of our Wi-Fi management system, we know when someone needs a visit and often have the solution in hand on our way to the room." This guest communication platform has been so successful for Meissner that he's gone on to commercialize it for other hospitality businesses throughout Latin America and beyond. You can learn more about it at *www.satrails.com*.

As Pam Huff used to tell me, "It's great to recover well. However, you always want to strive for flawless, uninterrupted service." When you do achieve that, it may be time for a standing ovation!

Questions for Discussion

- What's our process for collecting and processing client feedback?
- Do our team members know how to recover with style?
- What can we do today to ensure we turn unhappy customers into happy customers?

CHAPTER SIX

Standing Ovations for Your Staff

Often, I am asked, "How do we get people who have never *received* red-carpet customer service to *give* red-carpet customer service?" The answer, of course, is to model it for them by providing your employees with a little five-star treatment of their own. Those who have read my first book, *The Celebrity Experience*, or heard me deliver a keynote presentation know that my definition of red-carpet customer service is treating the person in front of you right now as if he or she were the most important person in the room. This is as true of how you treat your internal customers (your team members and coworkers) as it is of others you serve.

Larry Sternberg, president of Talent Plus, agrees: "What comes to mind, for me, very fundamentally, is the notion of significance, which is a very basic human need. When you give someone a gesture of appreciation in some way, among other things, what you're saying is 'You are a significant person and you are making a difference.' Personally, I view recognition, essentially, as helping people realize their significance."

In addition to giving red-carpet standing ovations to guests and new hires (see Chapter 1), the team at Talent Plus does many things to keep the applause going long beyond the first day:

✓ **Talent Plus has electronic greetings.** In addition to the red-carpet welcome, new employees and guests are welcomed by an electronic sign bearing their name.

✓ **Talent Plus has "Focus on You."** When new members of the team start working for Talent Plus, they participate in an activity called "Focus on You." It's a structured exercise in which the most senior leaders in the company sit down with their newest associates for an hour and a half and get to know them. New associates can ask the leadership team any question they want, both personal and professional. The leadership team spends the time exploring the interests of their new hires. Says Larry, "I don't know of any organization where new employees get to sit down with owners and other senior leaders on their first day. We all have only 24 hours in a day. When the senior leaders of an organization look forward to investing time in that new associate, it sends the message: *You are a significant person.*"

✓ **At Talent Plus, they celebrate with food.** Breakfast and lunch are provided by a chef. Breakfast is a healthy selection of fruit, yogurt, boiled eggs. "On Wednesdays," confides Larry, "we have waffles! Whatever diet anyone happens to be on, I assure you, they can go through our buffet line and have a delicious meal that fits the bill. Breaking bread together goes back to the dawn of time. If you know your guests and you know what they like, you have probably prepared something for them. That is part of rolling out the red carpet for anyone—be it customer or employee. Give them good food!"

✓ **Talent Plus is a three-story building with one coffee pot.** "That's because our founders believed that was a good way to gather: through food and drink," explains Cydney Koukol, chief communication officer. "If we had coffee pots on every floor, there would be people I would never see. It's a nice way for us to touch base with people."

✓ **Talent Plus has cocktail hour.** On the afternoon of an employee's first day, their Great Take Off Day, Talent Plus holds a cocktail reception at 4:30 p.m. All associates are invited to attend and are served heavy hors d'oeuvres prepared by the Talent Plus chef, with beer, wine, and soft drinks. Often spouses, parents, and children of the new associates also attend. "Whoever they would like to share it with is invited to come," says Larry.

✓ **Talent Plus gives out talent cards**. These documents are written in a way that is unique to each individual. "One of our analysts, with great care, creates this card unique to each new person," explains Larry. "It's in a frame, and we all display them on our desks." The Talent Card has three sections: "We like you because..." "You have these strengths..." and "Here is what we expect of you...."

Each section is customized for the recipient. The card is signed by the Talent Plus founders and presented to each new associate at the cocktail reception. (They also give them to clients after they have assessed them.) "This is a major deposit into someone's emotional bank account," says Larry. "Again, it makes that person feel significant, particularly because his/her family and friends have been invited to this event. They are always blown away because most of them work somewhere and they know other organizations just don't do this."

✓ **Talent Plus gives five-star cards.** These are about the size of a small postcard. They are provided to everyone on the team for the purpose of writing notes of appreciation to each other. "There are no rules around this," explains Larry. "Recognition programs, in most organizations, are still hierarchical." In other words, supervisors can write notes of recognition to their direct reports. "At Talent Plus, and at our client companies, anyone can write a note to anyone (s)he darned well pleases. The note is hand-delivered. It doesn't go in their personnel file. It's a note from one person to another."

The team at Talent Plus encourages clients to implement a similar practice, naming the card something that fits their culture. If one of their clients achieves something outstanding, they will blow up a card to 11 inches by 14 inches or even bigger. The note of appreciation is signed by everyone in the company.

✓ **Talent Plus sends notes to parents**. Says Larry, "We have an associate who has demonstrated notable leadership in the Lincoln community. She is the president of an organization that has, over the last few years, raised half a million dollars for a worthy charity. I wrote a note to her parents and said that I wanted to tell them how proud of the leadership their daughter had exercised in the community of Lincoln, Nebraska."

✓ **Talent Plus does "Plays of the Day."** Each morning the team at Talent Plus meets for Formation. One of the elements of that meeting is called "Plays of the Day." Anyone in the meeting can call out recognition to anyone else in the meeting. "We typically give out several of those on any given day," says Larry. "People also give out recognition to their family members: *My daughter just won the* *swim meet!* or *My son was just accepted for this school organization!* Whatever it may be."

✓ **Talent Plus leaves the bureaucracy to others**. "I hope what you're getting," says Larry, "is that it is very non-programmatic. It's very non-bureaucratic. It's very human. One human being recognizing another human being."

✓ **Talent Plus has career investment discussions**. There are no performance evaluations at Talent Plus. Instead they have career investment discussions. "These discussions are not about your performance. It's about how I— your supervisor—can celebrate your successes. How can I invest in you?" One of the questions is "Is there anything you would like to learn? How much time are you spending doing things you are good at and enjoy?" If the response doesn't land on a great number on the scale, the follow-up question is "How can I help you move that number up so you are spending more time at things you are good at and enjoy?" "The important thing about these career investment discussions," says Larry, "is acting as soon as the discussion is over. I remember having one of these discussions, during the recession, with someone who reported to me. She said, 'One of the things I would like to do is talk to the CEO of another company and see what they're thinking about right now.' It tickled me, because in less than 30 minutes, I handed her the name of a CEO and her phone number, and said, 'She'd really like to talk to you.'"

✓ **Talent Plus emotionally rehires their team.** "When you tell one of your associates," says Larry, "by note or face-to-face, that you appreciate the contributions he has made; that you are glad she is here; and that you are thankful for that person—when you say that to someone, you have emotionally rehired him/her. It's no different from telling your spouse on your anniversary that (s)he is the most important person in your life and how thankful you are that you've found him/her. You have just emotionally remarried your spouse."

Wow! Don't you want to work for that company? Maybe you could become your own version of Talent Plus and the other companies featured in this book. Having spent quite a bit of time talking with some members of the leadership team at Talent Plus, I suspect this is just the tip of the iceberg, and that were you to visit their offices, you'd find a group of people doing what they were meant to be doing, loving their jobs, and feeling valued and appreciated.

Before we move on to a company that accomplishes the same goals but with a different twist, let me tell you about an activity Larry has done with his team. It's worth thinking about the next time you feel you don't have time to give standing ovations to your staff:

When someone takes the time to prepare a hand written note, it shows that the recipient is significant and worth the investment. Yesterday, in a program I was leading, I explained what our five-star notes are and handed one out to each person in the group. I asked them to write one to someone. It doesn't matter who it is. Just write one to someone you feel deserves it. What they don't know is that I'm timing them. When the last person has finished his or her note, I stop my stopwatch. Yesterday was 100-percent typical. There were five people writing these notes. The longest was three and a half minutes. This is very, very economical and doesn't demand much time. One of the women in the program worked for an organization that employed 50 managers. If everyone one of them took three and a half minutes once a week, you'd have 2,500 notes a year that are tangible evidence of what you're doing in terms of positive reinforcement and recognition. The key is to be genuine and specific. I always end my notes with this four word sentence: "I'm glad you're here."

Does Your Company Need a Mayor?

G Adventures is a Toronto-based company focused on small-group adventure travel. The company operates on seven continents with 1,500 full time employees in 109 countries all around the world. When you're traveling with G Adventures, you're traveling with a group of about 10 to 14 people. They are proud to be about small groups and culture immersion wherever they go. They have more than 650 different itineraries and trips that they define by travel style (as opposed to geographical location). This ensures they have the right trip, and the right amount of adventure, for everyone.

G Adventures may be all about adventure travel. However, it's pretty certain that working for them is quite an adventure, as well. Here are just a few things they do to create an extraordinary experience for their staff members:

✓ **G Adventures has a mayor.** "I'm the Mayor of G
   Adventures," proclaims Dave Holmes. "I've been the mayor
   for about a year and a half now. It's undoubtedly the best
   job in the world." As mayor, Dave is part of a team called
   G Force. "It's our job to make sure our employees are as
   happy and engaged as possible," he explains. Externally, he
   speaks at conferences, travel shows, and trade shows, and
   is the voice of its employees all around the world.

✓ **G Adventures has 800 CEOs.** "Being a customer-
   obsessed company," explains Dave, "we consider our
   customer-facing employees the most important [people]
   in the company. This is why our founder, Bruce Poon Tip,
   gave up his CEO title about seven years ago. He decided

185

that he was no longer the most important person in our company because he rarely gets face-to-face contact with our travelers. Our 800 CEOs, otherwise known as chief experience officers, are tour guides, in-house, and home-base employees. They see customers every day, live and breathe our core values, and keep promises to our customers that we are going to change their lives through travel. They are the most important people in our company."

✓ **G Adventures has a zombie apocalypse.** Twice a year Bruce, the founder of G Adventures, chooses team members at random from different levels of the company, across the organization, from all over the world. If you are chosen, you get an e-mailed invitation from the "zombie master" with a message that reads: "This is top secret. Do not tell anyone." You are given instructions on when to show up at the airport, what to bring, and that's it. You have no idea where you're going. "I've been lucky enough to go on two," Dave tells me enthusiastically. During a zombie apocalypse you're flown somewhere to brainstorm ideas for three to five days in an exotic location. "You are in a boardroom for a lot of the time, solving a problem, or trying to come up with the next great thing, but there's always time for fun at night," says Mayor Dave.

✓ **G Adventures has a William Shatner meeting room.** Why wouldn't you want to have a meeting room decorated with the USS Enterprise and a cutout of William Shatner and Leonard Nimoy?

✓ **G Adventures hosts games like The Amazing G Race.** "We have a lot of creative fun at work," says Dave. "But if you are out in the field, you're not experiencing the home office. We wanted to create the same fun experience virtually. We do that by coming up with fun and

186

innovative ways to engage our employees through G
Nation (Salesforce technology they use to stay in touch
with their global workforce). "One of the things going on
right now is the Amazing G Race," comments Dave. "It's
a month-long scavenger hunt that presents a set of eleven
weekly challenges, weighted in difficulty. We took the
entire company of 1,500 people and assigned them each to
one of five teams. So that person you're sitting beside at an
office? Chances are you won't be on his team. It's a great
way to foster engagement around the world and to connect people with coworkers they might not otherwise have
the chance to know."

✓ **G Adventures has G-stock.** It's their big company gath-
ering. About 200 people from outside North America get
a chance to win their way to G-stock. They win golden
tickets to come to Toronto for a week. It culminates in a
three-day celebration at Niagara Falls where Bruce, the
founder, gives a full-day presentation talking about the
direction of the company for the next year.

✓ **G Adventures has swag bags.** "We have someone whose
background is in merchandising and swag," says Dave.
"She gets all the swag for our employees around the world.
We have everything for every kind of climate. Part of coming to G-stock is that you get your swag bag!"

✓ **G Adventures has a G apprentice program.** This
incentive program provides opportunities for G Adventure
staff to develop themselves in really fun ways.

✓ **G Adventures has haircuts and hot dogs.** This is the
day they hire a hot dog vendor to come and cook lunch for
all of the staff at Basecamp (the home office in Toronto).
Explains Dave, "We bring in three barbers and four hair-
stylists to give everyone a free haircut."

✓ **G Adventures has beer o'clock.** That's right. On Fridays at 4 o'clock, beer, wine, and cider appear in the refrigerator in the "bitchin' kitchen." There's ice cream and popcorn, too. It's part of their "happiness as a business model."

✓ **G Adventures has prom.** This past year, they invited people to dress up as they did at their high school prom and attend G prom. They went to a concert venue where they heard a live band play, handed out promo awards, and had an amazing time.

✓ **G Adventures has a ball pit.** In fact, the last stop before you are hired is an interview in the ball pit. You spin the wheel to determine the interview questions. What a great way to determine fit! If you don't like the ball pit, you're probably not a fit for the G Adventures culture.

✓ **G Adventures has purpose camps.** "We go to different places in the world where we have CEOs and, in some cases, staff and we take them offsite for four days to talk a lot more about the purpose of the company. We don't talk nuts and bolts," explains Mayor Dave, "but about the bigger philosophical stuff about what makes G Adventures so special and why the job they do is important."

Don't you want to work in a place that has a William Shatner meeting room? Don't you want to be part of a company that has swag bags and zombie apocalypses? I do!

Admit it. You secretly do, too.

Lest you think this is all fun and games, consider this: G Adventures has seen double-digit growth every single year they've been in business. Bruce Poon Tip founded the company as a solo entrepreneur in 1990, using two credit cards. He now has a team of 1,500 people committed to the idea that travel could be the greatest form of wealth distribution the world has ever seen. They are passionate about the fact

that when you travel with G Adventures, most of your money stays local and benefits local economies. They are committed to changing people's lives through travel.

"What we do for our employees is not cheap," says Mayor Dave. "We invest a lot of money in making our employees happy, but we have always seen results because of it!"

Or Maybe You Need a Culture Fairy

"We always have our employees in mind because we, like you, believe that, if our employees are happy, it turns into our customers being happy," Katie Fronk of Davinci Office Solutions told me. "They'll be able to feel that our employees love working here and love their jobs." Davinci Virtual Office Solutions is a global provider of business addresses, live answering services, and meeting space for entrepreneurs, small businesses, and independent professionals. They are headquartered in Salt Lake City, Utah, and have partners at more than 1,000 locations worldwide. Katie works in their home office in Utah.

Davinci is another organization that has discovered that the solution to customer happiness is employee happiness. Here are just a few things they do to give their 107 team members an extraordinary experience:

✓ **Davinci has a culture fairy.** This is Katie Fronk's official title. Like Mayor Dave at G Adventures, her responsibility is to ensure a positive company culture and keep employees happy. She is also the HR manager, but she adds, "I don't like to be called that. I do have some HR responsibilities, but my primary role is to sprinkle fairy dust on the staff and make sure we're all having fun and that company morale is high." Katie also has a "mini-fairy" who works in her department and helps her with this mission.

✓ **Davinci has five employees of the month.** Employee recognition is a huge priority at Davinci, and they aren't stingy about it. Rather than celebrate one employee monthly, they honor five. Anyone on the team can nominate someone who has done a great job on a project, gone above and beyond, or received positive feedback from a client. These employees of the month are announced at a management meeting to a thunderous round of applause. "We read the nominations aloud so the honorees know why they were awarded. We don't just give them the award and we're done," says Katie. "We really celebrate them as team members." The chosen five get trophies and a night at the movies together along with the culture fairy and her mini-fairy. "They love it because it's a night out as team members and it's fun," she enthuses.

✓ **They have Davinci University.** One of the core values at Davinci is the pursuit of learning and growth. So each month they host a class for employees. It is given during the day or after work hours, depending on schedules and what's going on in the company. Topics include everything from health (Zumba or dance classes) and customer service (empathy and compassion or de-escalating angry callers), to general life skills (budgeting and finance). The speakers are sometimes outside presenters. At other times, they are Davinci management or staff members.

✓ **At Davinci, they lunch with the boss.** "Many of us have worked for companies where the main boss is not a part of the team. Our bosses have always said, "We want to know our employees and be part of the team." They are with us every single day. They know us by name and participate in our work life," explains the culture fairy. One way they accomplish this is to host lunch once or twice a month for different employees. New hires are immediately invited. Then participation is rotated, so it's always a different mix of people. "The employees love it!" she adds.

✓ **Davinci has team-building events.** "Getting together outside of the work environment builds relationships, so this is a huge deal for us," says Katie. Every few months, they do something different—such as a baseball game or a family barbeque in the park. They've even created their own Davinci Amazing Race. (Anyone starting to think the culture fairy and Mayor Dave should get together? Hmmm!)

✓ **Davinci celebrates reaching goals.** Each department at Davinci sets its own company goals. Departments compete with each other for the top score. The top winner of each department gets a bonus check and breakfast cooked by the one and only culture fairy, with help from her mini-fairy.

✓ **Davinci has personality.** In addition to the company core values, the team at Davinci has defined five personality traits they ask their employees to demonstrate in

191

their interactions with customers and coworkers. "The core values are the standards we live by," says Katie. "The personality traits are who we are. We want anyone we meet to use these words to describe us because this is who we are. The personality traits of the Davinci team are: alive, driven, bold, fresh, and compassionate. They have a recognition program that allows for anyone to nominate a Davinci employee just for demonstrating one of the personality traits. The nominees get Davinci swag such as pens and T-shirts. Once they've been nominated for all five traits, they become part of the Davinci elite. "They are basically the superstars who have really shown they have embraced our personality traits and live our brand," explains Katie.

All that fairy dust must be working. Davinci has been named one of the 500 fastest-growing companies by *Inc.* magazine, in 2010 and 2012, as well as one of the 50 fastest-growing companies in Utah.

Celebrate Your League of Superheroes

When it comes to creating a culture where employees feel appreciated and inspired, it's no surprise that Ruby Receptionists tops the list of great places to work. In 2014 they came in as number three on *Fortune Magazine's* Best Small Company to Work for in the United States, for their third year in a row to appear in the top three spots. In 2015, they landed in the top 10 Best Large Companies to Work for in Oregon, as identified by *Oregon Business Magazine*. Here are just a few of the ways they create a culture that keeps their employees falling in love with Ruby:

✓ **Ruby Receptionists has fashion Fridays.** One of the values at Ruby Receptionists is to create community. One of the ways they live this is by "sharing special times together." To that end, they have a fun, end-of-the-week ritual formerly called "not-so-casual-Friday" (now called "fashion Friday"). Each Friday, they choose a theme, and rather than come dressed in jeans or "dressed down," team members show up in costume. Some favorite themes include "dress like a kid," "dress like your favorite video game character," and "bring a bad hair day to work." What rituals could you create that promote your company culture and fun at work?

✓ **At Ruby Receptionists, they appreciate big and correct small.** Employee appreciation is one of Kendra Neal's biggest tools for inspiring her team to work hard and provide great service. She believes in appreciating big and correcting small. "When I've got the whole group in front of me," she says, "I waste no time telling them how great they are! Together we are the new frontier of world-class

service and the best customer service team in the nation. Then, when someone makes a misstep and doesn't quite live up to our standard of service, I address it one-on-one with that person and make sure they have the tools they need to succeed in the future." Because Kendra is so appreciative, she has an incredibly dedicated team who hold themselves to a high standard. "It doesn't take much to tell some, 'You didn't quite hit the mark here.'" Kendra says, "They immediately recognize it as an opportunity to grow and we easily move on."

✓ **At Ruby Receptionists, they personalize appreciation.** Inspired by the book *The 5 Languages of Appreciation in the Workplace,* by Gary Chapman and Paul White, Kendra tries to personalize her approach to appreciation. She and her team at Ruby Receptionists took the assessments provided on Chapman's and White's Website. She learned that, unlike herself, most of her team feels most appreciated when they are verbally praised. So she changed her approach and spends much more time telling them how much they are valued than she did before.

✓ **At Ruby Receptionists, they express thanks in a close-up.** Recently, when they did an amazing job reaching one of their goals, Ruby Receptionists CEO Jill Nelson wanted to know what she could do to appreciate them. Kendra suggested she record herself on video with an expression of thanks and "way to go" for the team. "She did and they loved it. Of course, in typical Jill fashion, she took it one step further and gave us a nice catered lunch, as well!"

✓ **Ruby has superhero meetings:** Once a quarter, Kendra and her Ruby leadership team stay out on the floor and handle the workload while their league of super heroes have their own two-hour meeting. They set their own agenda and have discussions that they may not want to bring up in a meeting with the director of their department present. They come out with notes and ideas that help us continue to improve the experience for our customers and out team!

✓ **Ruby Receptionists has superhero analogy.** "By the way," says Kendra, "there's a reason why we at Ruby Receptionists look at ourselves as a league of superheroes. In the movie *The Avengers*, you don't have 10 Hulks or 10 Ironmen. Everybody has a different superpower and they complement each other. This is true in the workplace, as well. You need someone who is great at calming down upset clients; someone who's great at importing a spreadsheet; some who's great at nurturing a new account; someone who's great at follow-through; etc. We consider ourselves a league of super heroes because we each have different strengths and want to find a way to support the team with those strengths."

✓ **Ruby shares superhero stories.** Kendra keeps a space on the team SharePoint site for superhero stories. "We have a graphic of the Ruby cartoon girl as a superhero. She's our client happiness mascot. We even made T-shirts and she's standing on top of a taco" (because Ruby Super Heroes love tacos!). At the top of the Web page it reads, "This is the place for you to brag shamelessly about the truly exquisite caliber of work you do every day!" Any time a Ruby problem solver feels she did a great job on a project or with a client interaction, she tells the story on SharePoint. Each Wednesday, at their weekly meeting, Kendra chooses the one that speaks to her the most and recognizes that person in front of Ruby peers. "It's fun for them and fun for me!" she exclaims.

This is only scratching the surface. For many other inspirational ideas and tips, visit the Ruby blog on the company's Website.

Give Them Their Chicken Soup

Doug Conant, the former CEO of Campbell's Soup, is known for turning the company around after a dramatic market decline. Doug maintained a practice of hand-writing thank-you notes to team members daily. During the course of his time at Campbell's, Conant wrote out 30,000 thank-you notes to his employees. The company employed only 20,000 people. "I made it personal," Conant said, noting that a near-death car accident a few years ago made him the recipient of thousands of notes from his colleagues. Notes expressed how much the team was there for Conant, just as much as he had been there for them. Today, as Founder and CEO of ConantLeadership, Doug Conant continues his excellent practice of writing thank-you notes.

Take the $100 Challenge

When Paul Greenberg, CEO of *Nylon* magazine, brought a group of 10 employees together and stood in front of them alongside the VP of television and video, Shruti Ganguly, the group didn't know what to expect. "Are we fired?" one of them asked. "Uh, no," replied Paul. Instead, Greenberg took out 10 100-dollar bills and handed them out to each team member. You might be thinking, *Now that's the kind of meeting I'd like to have with my boss.* However, Greenberg quickly explained that the $100 was not theirs to keep. Instead, he and Ganguly were sending them out to do something good for someone else.

"Over breakfast one day, Director Vince Peone was telling me some of his ideas. These were ideas he had pitched to others, to no avail," explains Shruti. "One of them was a version of the $100.00 challenge, except with strangers. It was a slightly different version than the one we ended up doing." Ganguly mentioned it to Greenberg, who liked the idea of doing something good for someone else and said, "Let's make it internal!"

None of the 10 employees knew what was coming. "Authenticity means a lot to us at *Nylon*," says Shruti. So when you see the employees' surprised faces on the video, those are real. In fact, they were all working under deadline because their print issue was closing. Anyone could have said, "No. I can't do this now." However, they didn't. When Shruti asked, "Do you accept the $100 challenge?" the answer was a resounding yes!

✓ The 10 employees paired up and hit the streets of New York City. Some were followed by cameras and others brought their own iPads along to capture the moment. Their acts of generosity and kindness ranged from giving big tips to a taxi driver and a waitress in a diner, to donating money to animal shelters, to handing out $100 worth of socks and $100 worth of pizza to people living in a homeless shelter. A couple of people just stood on the street corner and gave away money. Or tried to. "I actually want to release an unedited version of the video," exclaims Shruti. "We were standing there for so long trying to give away money and people just wouldn't take it." One particularly moving part of the challenge was when Daniel, a *Nylon* employee, befriended a homeless man who was sketching and complained of the cold. Daniel returned with gloves, sketch pads, colored pencils, and cash. You can see the gratitude in the man's eyes. In fact, why don't you watch? You can find the video here: *https://youtu.be /glwjyg3JuQs.*

Although their acts of generosity certainly helped many people that day, more importantly, the $100 challenge affected the morale of those involved. "I've never encountered an experience like this," said Daniel. "This changed my life."

What about you? Will you #TakeThe100 DollarChallenge?

Commitment to Employees and Community

A few years ago, in 2009, I was working with Penn National Gaming to develop its red-carpet customer service training. Around that same time, their pavilion and restaurant areas at their casino in Joliet, Illinois, was devastated by a fire. Although it took three months to rebuild the casino, the company's commitment to employees at the time was so impressive, I asked them to share the story with you. Here's what they said.

✓ In March 2009, Empress Casino was devastated by a fire that destroyed the casino's entire pavilion area, including all restaurants and office space. Penn National Gaming committed to reopening the casino within 90 days of the fire. During the period in which the casino was closed, Penn National Gaming continued to pay Empress employees their full salary and benefits as well as 50 percent of employees' reported tip income. "While our employees were off work, we thought it would be a great time to give back to the community," said a Maggie Deering, HR manager for the casino. "In the 90-day period when we were closed, our employees logged more than 5,000 volunteer hours to help local organizations." Within three months Empress reopened with a temporary entrance and food outlets. In December 2010 they opened their brand new pavilion with new restaurants and were renamed Hollywood Casino Joliet. At their grand reopening, they rolled out the red carpet for all their guests.

Start-Up Budget? Use Your Points!

✓ Apryl DeLancey is the president of Social Age Media. In the company's first few months, she wanted to show her team how much she appreciated them, but she was working within a startup budget. She cashed in her points from American Express to buy Zappos gift cards, treating each person to a new pair of Vans sneakers. The themes of the shoes were Star Wars or the Beatles, depending on the recipient. She put them in a gift bag along with other smaller trinkets that matched the recipient's personality. Then, she took her employees out for a thank-you breakfast and presented them with their surprise gifts!

Lobstah, Anyone?

When Carol Gee, author of *The Venus Chronicles*, worked in the Rollins School of Public Health at Emory University in Atlanta, Georgia, her supervisor was a physician and scientist and a typical type-A personality. Says Carol, "She was smart, intense, and slept only three or four hours a night. I was a female, master's degree–level military vet. It made us a great team. She would think of ideas and I would execute them." She kept Carol working at a fast pace, but was always very appreciative.

✓ On her birthday Carol's boss came in and told her to take the following day off and added, "Make sure you're home to receive something." Carol spent the next day at her house. She wasn't sure what to expect when a UPS man arrived at her doorstep carrying a large box. "I had no idea what was in the box, but whatever it was, it was moving!" Then she saw the label on the box which read, "Lobsters from Maine: Live Animals." When her husband, a food service professional, came home, they opened the container. "I had never seen anything like this in my life," Carol exclaimed. Inside, they found a huge pot with a lid, butter, bibs, crackers, tongs, and a couple of lobsters on ice. It was everything you'd need for a lobster dinner. Another professor had gifted Carol with a bottle of merlot. "I had lobster and I had wine," she enthused. "Life was good!"

The Purple Sheep Award

Rhonda Osborne, RN, CEO of Hospice of Marshal County, explains the meaning behind their Purple Sheep award:

Approximately eight years ago, I read an article by Seth Godin, "Purple Cow: Transform Your Business by Being Remarkable." He stated that if a person saw a purple cow in a pasture, it would certainly stand out from all the rest. He used that analogy, encouraging business leaders to find ways to make their company remarkable—a purple cow in their industry—to stand out from all the rest. This was about the time HMC had a significant increase in competitors. I spent time trying to think how HMC could be that purple cow in our area. This was also during the planning phase for our inpatient hospice facility, Shepherd's Cove. With some time, the concept of the purple cow was transformed to a purple sheep to align with naming of Shepherd's Cove and as a mechanism to recognize staff. Families served by HMC and Shepherd's Cove are provided with a form in their family packet of hospice information to use to recognize staff that render remarkable service. An HMC volunteer designed a "Purple Sheep Award." Staff members covet the purple sheep. The simple award is displayed with great honor in their cubicles or on their desks. We took this idea one step further. We already had in place the "And Then Some Award," [in which] peers can recognize their coworkers for doing their job "and then some" more. These recipients receive a lilac sheep. These, as well, are displayed with pride.

Letters to the Family

Dave Timmons is a senior sales trainer for Raymond James and Associates in St. Petersburg, Florida. The following story hearkens back to his days as a senior vice president for Bank of America.

✓ "In this particular role," says Dave, "I had eight people working for me. One time, I asked one of my team who, for the sake of this book, we'll call Joanna, to head a special two-month-long project. She finished the project under budget, way ahead of schedule, and exceeded my expectations. So I wanted to do something special to thank her." Dave uses a special form to get to know team members, asking them to share 10 of their favorite things (favorite foods, restaurant, shopping center, and so on); or some of their firsts (first car, first concert, and so on) "I knew Joanna had a sports team she liked and particular places she liked to shop. However, I wanted to make this recognition extra special because she really deserved it." About a month after she completed the project, a letter showed up in Joanna's mailbox addressed to her husband, Roger; and their three children, Emily, Shaun and Katrina. It read,

"Dear Roger, Emily, Shaun, and Katrina: I want to tell you how special your wife and mother is. She just finished a project and she is so appreciated at our company that I wanted you to know two things: First, how proud we are of her and how appreciative I am to you for allowing her to take time away from you to work for us. On behalf of me and our entire team, please surprise her with this gift certificate from Ann Taylor Loft, because we know that's where she likes to shop. Sincerely, Dave Timmons, Senior Vice President."

✓ I can only imagine what dinner was like the night she came home from work and Roger and the children had something to share with her. Says Dave, "She came in the next day crying about how important it was to include her family in her job success.... When you engage the people [employees] care about, like their family, in their success, you hit a double home run. You can reward them with something—and that's good. But if you want to go for the real *wow*, try to include their family. It especially gives the kids something nice to remember."

Dave is also a wonderful professional speaker and has given keynote presentations all over the country. Like me, Dave finds that his audience members are often the richest source of great stories. Dave recalls one of these instances:

I was speaking for an ink and color printer company in Flint, Michigan. After my presentation, a gentleman named Chris came up to chat, as people will often do. At around 30 years old, he was the youngest regional manager in this company and reported directly to the president of his division. Chris and his wife had recently had their first child, whom they named Johnny. A few days after Johnny was brought home, a...manila envelope appeared in their mailbox. It was addressed to Johnny. This is just one of the coolest things. It gives me goosebumps! It didn't have a return address or anything, so Chris's wife waited until he got home and they opened it together. There was a beautiful, handwritten note on the stationary belonging to the company Chris worked for, and signed by his boss, David, the president of the division. It read: "Dear Johnny— Welcome to the world! I want you to know how special your father is to our company and what a great Dad he's going to be for you." It went on to say some really nice things specifically about Chris and about his integrity, character, work ethic, and all these things you want your child to understand when they are old enough to comprehend. The end of the note read: "Johnny, attached to this letter is a job application for our company. I want you to know that when you are ready to work for us, you have a job. So please keep this for when you are ready to write and ready to work and we will hire you!"

Isn't that the coolest thing you've ever heard of? I mean, can you imagine? I'm guessing they probably framed the letter and showed it to everybody that ever came over to their house. They probably told everyone. What a neat way to recognize and employee and do it through his new son. Just incredible!

I would have to agree.

Simple Standing Os

Here are some easy-to-implement ideas that other leaders have used to show appreciation to their staff members:

- ✓ One of my past clients held what they called gag awards, giving humorous recognition for the foibles and funnies that happened to employees throughout the year.

✓ Nido Qubein, president of High Point University, personally calls staff and faculty members on their birthdays.

✓ A staff and faculty member is highlighted in each issue of *High Point University Magazine.*

✓ The supervisors at Durham Performing Arts Center are equipped with spotlight cards. When they see someone going above and beyond, they give that person a card. Team members save them up and trade them in for gifts and prizes.

✓ Janet Hessenflow, executive director of Crossroads Hospice in Missouri, holds an annual team retreat every year. The retreat is always fun. As an added bonus, Janet hires masseuses to give attendees chair massages during the event. With up to 500 people in attendance, the 12 paid masseuses keep busy throughout the event. The employees love it!

✓ People's Bank of Commerce in Minnesota uses the "Give a WOW!" peer-to-peer recognition program offered by Terryberry.com. This program allows them to connect with their 70 employees through an online, social media–style program that celebrates and values their success in modeling the bank's vision, mission, and core values. The bank has more than 80 engagements per week, with strong participation levels year after year. Terryberry.com is a 97-year-old provider of recognition programs, products, and services to 25,000 companies and organizations throughout North America and Europe.

✓ When STARS (employees) of the Gaylord Opryland Hotel are recognized for a job well done by one of their guests, they are praised by their leaders and given a round of applause from their coworkers

✓ In addition to going through an extensive orientation program on the hotel's service basics, the new STARS of the Gaylord Opryland Resort are invited back in 90 days for a refresher. This also gives the leadership team time to get additional feedback on what's working and what's not.

"Donna, We Love You!" Day

One of my dear friends, Dawn Winder, also happens to be my former boss, and one of my favorite bosses and people of all time. I haven't worked for her in about 16 years, but we are still friends and she continues to be my inspiration. When I left her employment to begin my career as a professional speaker, she and my other coworkers gave me a true red-carpet sendoff. This story was originally published in a book by International speaker and author Barbara Glanz (*www.barbaraglanz.com*) titled *Handle With CARE: Motivating and Retaining Employees. Creative, Low-Cost Ways to Raise Morale, Increase Commitment, and Reduce Turnover* (McGraw Hill, 2002).

For two years, I had been the activities director at Park Place, a large retirement community for seniors. It was a wonderful place to work, and I was tremendously close to our residents and my fantastic team of coworkers. Nevertheless, I was being led to begin my own speaking and performing business, a dream I'd had for many years.

✓ The night before my last day on the job, my boss asked if I would come in a bit late the next day. I enjoyed sleeping in and then headed off to work. When I arrived, more than 150 residents, all the department heads, my employees, and other team members were all lining the hallway, greeting me as I came in. The lobby was filled with the many faces I had grown to love over the past two years. They were all applauding—for me! I could barely stop my tears from flowing as I was escorted down the hallway and into the lobby, where I was approached by our newly elected president of the resident council. With tears in *his* eyes, he presented me with a framed document which he read aloud:

Proclamation

Whereas

Donna Cutting

Has been our Activities Director and endeared herself to all by her warm, caring attitude, her professional competence, her tact and expertise and

Whereas

Donna is leaving us to follow her lifelong dream in another endeavor, be it Resolved

Though we are saddened by her departure and will miss her cheerful smile, her careful planning and her marvelous voice, we wish her every success in this new phase of her life. In appreciation for her devotion to our needs we affirm and proclaim, May 14, 1999 to be

Donna, We Love You! Day

The Resident Council of Park Place of Clearwater Retirement Residence

It was signed by every member of the resident council.

✓   I was presented with this beautiful plaque and was the recipient of many wonderful words and warm hugs as I was escorted into our ice cream parlor. There, the department head team and my own employees had set up a beautiful and scrumptious homemade breakfast in my honor. In addition to all of this, they gave me a gift of some magnificent wind chimes, a whimsical gift in honor of my new company, which was then called "Whimsical Notions." My own staff members, Paul and Noel, also gifted me with a beautiful black handbag.

✓ Throughout the entire day, residents and staff alike would stop me in the hallways, the elevators, and the activities room to say, "We love you, Donna!" Even residents who had *never* attended an activity in the years I'd worked there stopped me with hugs to say, "We love you, Donna!"

It truly was "Donna, We Love You!" Day.

That plaque is hanging on my wall. The wind chimes sing on my porch. The bag was filled with my business tools for many years. The memories of the people of Park Place are in my heart. I love them, too!

The 21 Days of Thank You

Dawn Winder serves as the community director of Allegro in Tarpon Springs, a senior living community. "We decided we're going to do 'The 21 Days of Thank You,'" she wrote to me in an e-mail. "The 21 Days of Thank You is an exercise I encourage leaders to do. It provides one idea to show appreciation, every day, for 21 consecutive workdays. The point is: We sometimes get so busy in our day-to-day jobs that we forget to take the time to deliver little gestures of appreciation to our team."

I could tell Dawn was excited that she and her managers were going to put plan into action. (I was not surprised either. Dawn Winder taught me a great deal about employee appreciation and, in fact, is a direct contributor to "The 21 Days of Thank You." Many of these ideas are ones she gave me by modeling them at my former job. She was, incidentally, the kind of boss that you'd follow anywhere. Apparently, she still is.) I asked Dawn to keep me posted as she and her leadership team went through the process. Her follow-up e-mails delighted me:

"We made three people cry today," she wrote gleefully. (Obviously, she meant this in a good way!) "Beverly, our chef extraordinaire, returned from her lunch break to find her cooler covered with thank-you [sticky] notes! She said it really made her day...week...year! We also plastered the inside of the community bus for our driver of 12 years. He roared with laughter and blinked tears of appreciation. We're having a great time. The team building is an added bonus!"

A few days later I received another email from Dawn: "After the department heads and I finished painting the break room, we hung the chain of kindness [more on this on Day Five in the following list] so everyone could see! People really got engaged and were writing notes about each other all day long."

With such enthusiasm and dedication to giving standing ovations to their staff, is it any wonder that, based on anonymous surveys, longevity, and low turnover, Allegro of Tarpon Springs holds first place for employee satisfaction company-wide?

Following is the "21 Days of Thank You." (It is also available on my Website as a free download.) Again, it is designed for you to you take one action a day for 21 consecutive workdays. Some of the actions take a little preparation, so it's a good idea to plan ahead. If you follow through, let me know how it goes. If you do this as a team, meet regularly to share stories and celebrate!

- ✓ Day One: Send an e-mail thanking someone who makes a difference in your work life. Be sincere and very specific about what he/she does that you appreciate. Expect nothing in return. Just reach out and say "Thank you!"
- ✓ Day Two: Thank an employee or coworker face-to-face, telling him specifically how he makes a difference to your company and/or your workday. If you work alone, pick up the phone and talk to a coworker or leave a message.

✓ Day Three: Spend some time purposefully walking the floor. In the words of Ken Blanchard: "Catch someone doing something right." When you see it, say it—and give her on-the-spot, specific praise.

✓ Day Four: Plaster positive sticky notes everywhere. Gather a group of department heads and/or coworkers. Choose one employee you want to praise or encourage. Write positive messages on the notes and plaster them all over the employee's work area. Give someone a big visible *wow* and make his day. If you're a solo entrepreneur, choose five people you admire and write appreciative notes on their Facebook pages. (This tip was taken directly from Dawn herself. She did this for us all the time when I worked for her.)

✓ Day Five: Start a chain of kindness. On a paper "link" write specific words of praise about an employee or coworker. Share it with her so she can bask in your words for a moment. Now, give that employee or coworker a blank chain link and ask her to find someone else to praise and appreciate. And so on. Post the chain on the bulletin board and watch it grow as others pay it forward. Work alone? Do it on Facebook, or via e-mail, phone, or Twitter.

✓ Day Six: Encourage a team member who needs a little lift. Let him know how he makes a difference and what he does well. Ask whether he needs help or guidance, and provide it. Strive to have the team member leave the conversation feeling great about himself and his work. If you work alone, give someone you think could use a little lift or some support a call!

✓ Day Seven: Go on WOW patrol. Choose a team member who has really gone above and beyond. Put together a balloon bouquet and a special certificate. Gather that person's coworkers to help you surprise her with the WOW patrol. Share how she has made a difference, then applaud and celebrate. Present the balloons and certificate and take a group photo. (Work alone? Do this for a colleague and show up at her door!)

✓ Day Eight: Write a handwritten thank-you note to a team member or coworker, specifically stating how he makes a difference to the team and your workplace.

✓ Day Nine: Divide a piece of paper into two columns. In the first column, list the names of all your direct reports. In the second column, write something positive that each person contributes to the team. Leave no one out—even if you really have to work to find the positive. Carry that list with you for a week. When you have the opportunity, privately share the appropriate positive praise with each person on the list. Try to get through the entire list within a week.

✓ Day 10: Bring in treats to say thank you to the entire team. Bagels, pizza, cupcakes, and/or candy would be appreciated. If you prefer not to use food, purchase $1 lottery tickets for each staff member. Just be prepared to lose someone special if one of those lottery tickets is a big winner.

✓ Day 11: Visit with a new employee or coworker. Welcome her to the organization and invite her to have lunch with you. Introduce the newcomer to at least three other people. Follow up with a handwritten welcome note.

✓ Day 12: Find a staff member or coworker who does a lot behind the scenes without a whole lot of recognition. Let him know that you notice his contribution. Specifically point out how the little things he does make a big difference.

✓ Day 13: Gather your team for an impromptu stand-up meeting. Ask each person to spend 60 seconds sharing good news—personal or professional—with the team. Celebrate together and go back to work. If you already have a meeting scheduled for this day, begin or end the meeting with good news.

✓ Day 14: Have face-to-face meetings with at least two employees. Talk to them about their long-term goals. Where do they see themselves in five years? Consider where you might be able to encourage and mentor them. Think about what you might be able to delegate that would challenge them and help them along the path to their desired future.

✓ Day 15: If you work in a place that has second and third shifts, leave a thank-you note and possibly some treats for the people working one or both of those shifts. Or, write a thank-you note and provide a treat to someone who works in a different department. Be specific in your praise and let that person know how you appreciate the good work she is doing.

✓ Day 16: Give a standing ovation to someone who has gone above and beyond lately. Gather 10 or more coworkers to meet at a predetermined place and time. Arrange for the recipient to come by, then surprise him with a long-lasting, heartfelt standing ovation! Be sure to tell the recipient specifically what he did to warrant such a visible display of appreciation.

✓ Day 17: Surprise an employee with one of the following: let her leave a half hour early with pay; give her a long lunch and do that person's job yourself for an hour; or swap one task of her choice.

✓ Day 18: Start a "traveling trophy." Find something fun to use as a trophy. It could be a rubber chicken, a stuffed animal, or something humorous that goes along with your mission or brand. Give it to one of your team members and tell him specifically why he is the recipient of this award today. When an hour is up, the recipient needs to find someone else who makes a difference, and then pay it forward. Keep it going all day long and see who ends up with the trophy at the end of the day.

✓ Day 19: Write and deliver five applause certificates. Be very specific about how each person demonstrates the standards you hold for customer experience.

✓ Day 20: Have lunch with one or two of your direct reports. Ask for their opinions, no holds barred, about how things are going at work. What are their specific suggestions for improvement? Thank them for their input. During the course of the next week, try to implement at least two of their ideas. Be sure to give them credit.

✓ Day 21: Write a handwritten thank-you note to one of your employees who has really gone above and beyond lately. Instead of hand delivering it, send it via snail mail to his home.

Congratulations! You've completed the "21 Days of Thank You" challenge. Let this not be an end, but the beginning of an intentional, consistent practice of giving kudos to your staff. Read through this chapter again. Try some of the ideas others have shared. Add your own. Write to me and let me know how it's going. Who knows? Your standing ovations idea might just end up in my next book! Remember: When you roll out the red carpet for your team members, they are more likely to do the same for your customers.

Questions for Discussion

- Are we role modeling red carpet service for our staff?
- What ideas shall we implement to show appreciation?
- Who deserves our appreciation today?
- How will we show appreciation for the behind-the-scenes players?

CHAPTER SEVEN

Build Buzz With Social Media, Events, and Community Service

"Edith was really the original brander," remarks Susan Claasen, a professional actress and the artistic director of the Invisible Theatre in Tucson, Arizona. She's referring to renowned costume designer Edith Head, who provided costumes for 446 films and won eight Academy Awards. Susan should know. She spends much of her time bringing the icon to life in her touring one-woman show, *A Conversation With Edith Head.*

"She was doing the red carpet before Joan Rivers—may she rest in peace—was born, because that's what Hollywood costume designers did. She put a face on the profession. If she were alive today, she'd have the most popular and influential fashion blog around. She knew marketing," Susan continues. "She was syndicated in 35 or 40 magazines. This was unheard of at the time. Edith wanted to share her tricks with women and gentlemen everywhere. She was on television doing makeovers before the term was coined."

Today there are countless available platforms for creating red-carpet experiences for your customers. Best of all, when they are used effectively, you not only engage your fans but give them an easy way to rave about you and your company everywhere. Susan Claasen, much like Edith Head, is an expert at this. I met Susan when she brought her show to North Carolina Stage Company in Asheville, North Carolina. She was enthralling. I easily imagined myself in the presence of the legend herself. The experience did not end when Susan left the stage. When the audience reluctantly left their seats and went back to the lobby, we found that the red carpet was rolled out for us, and "Edith" was right there, waiting.

- ✓ In character, Susan posed with her fans on the carpet under a sign bearing the name of her show while "paparazzi" took photos. She and her team captured the e-mail addresses of fans, which helped build their list of contacts. After the show, they sent us each our photo with "Edith Head" and a personal note.

- ✓ During the show, Edith gently poked fun at a man in the audience, suggesting he might wear a bag over his head and that his outfit would not be "Edith-approved." That lucky gentleman got to pose with and without the bag over his head on the red carpet. Throughout the post-show, Edith made sassy comments about the outfits of audience members and presented each person with a gold sticker that read *Edith Head Approved*. I believe I even saw the man with the bag over his head sporting a sticker.

- ✓ Susan came up with this idea when she performed at the Edinborough Fringe Festival, a huge event with more than 2,000 different productions happening at the same time. "People from all over the world, who perhaps had never heard of Edith Head, wanted a sticker and a photo on the red carpet." Of course, the first thing I did when I received my photo was post it on social media. In fact, there's a photo of my Edith Head Approved sticker on my Facebook page, as well.

This chapter is filled with easy-to-implement ideas for creating literal and figurative red-carpet experiences that go viral. There are also tips for using unique marketing strategies, events, and community involvement to give back, engage customers, and build buzz about your business.

A Twitter Movie Moment

Realizing he had very little time to grab a bite on a travel day, Peter Shankman, speaker, media personality, and author of *Zombie Loyalists: Using Great Service to Create Rabid Fans* (St. Martins Press, 2015), sent this tweet out to Morton's Steakhouse, along with a smiley emoticon: *@Mortons can you meet me at the Newark Airport with a porterhouse when I land in 2 hours? K? Thanks!* Says Shankman, "I was joking. I expected only a laugh—not a steak."

✔ To his utter surprise, as he approached the driver waiting for him, he noticed a well-dressed representative of Morton's Steakhouse standing there with a bag. Alex from Morton's in Hackensack had driven 23 miles to deliver a full meal to Shankman, remarking, "I heard you were hungry." Peter, in his own words, was *floored*.

True, Mr. Shankman has more than 166,000 Twitter followers, and Mortons probably knew what great publicity they would create. But isn't that the point? Social media gives us a fantastic opportunity to create "movie moments" for our customers. Those "movie moments" become stories worth sharing!

Social Media That Creates Loyal Fans

Research done by Jay Baer and the Social Habit found that 53 percent of Americans who follow brands in social media are more loyal to those brands. This may be especially critical for companies that do most of their business online. Although technology has certainly opened up a variety of platforms, and changed the way business is done, the fact is: People still like doing business with people they like. Social media gives those organizations an opportunity to connect with customers on a more personal level, sharing the "personality" of their company with the world. For those of us in customer-facing positions, it's an opportunity to connect with people on a wider scale and keep the conversation going in between our in-person encounters.

✓ If there is a team of people who know how to harness the power of social media to serve customers, it's the team at Zappos. The company has a "social team" made up of 13 people monitoring various social platforms across content, strategy, and customer support. If you follow @Zappos _Service on Twitter, you'll notice team members signing on by name, to tell their customers and the Twitter universe about who is there, ready to help them. For instance, this tweet from July 4, 2015: *Happy 4th of July, everyone! Geoff here to hang out with you for the day! Let me hear about your plans! BBQ? Fireworks? Let me know.*

✓ Geoff, Michaela, and a number of other Zappos team members spend time on Twitter replying to customer tweets, resolving service issues, and generally tweeting fun photos and bits of trivia to engage with their fans. One recent tweet even centered on helping a customer find a dress that was sold elsewhere and showed up on someone else's Tumblr page. Says Aziz Bawany, social marketing lead for Zappos, "We also have third parties we contract to help us. We're trying to use as many tools as possible. It's so easy for things to slip by. We are passionate about serving our customers and addressing their needs."

✓ Aziz also suggests that you don't put any barriers on what happens on your social media platforms. Zappos team members have the freedom to create social media accounts that, to some degree, can speak for the company. "Your employees are really your best advocates. Given the opportunity, they will tell your story in a much greater way than any other planned marketing strategy. Build a good culture that's aware of and intelligent about how to use social media, and get your employees involved. We remind our team that they represent the company, and give them the proper channels to use if something goes wrong. Our strategy so far has been to tell them: *Be yourself; put a little thought into it; be true and be human.*"

✓ Aziz knows it's important to use a sense of humor on social media to create raving fans. "There was a time when high punk metal spikes were really popular again, including on shoes. One customer wrote (on social media), "This is terrible! Who would wear something like that?" I used it as an opportunity to make a joke, like, "There are a lot of things you can do! Like go out for a night on the town, use your shoe to tenderize a steak, use it pull a nail out of a piece of wood! It's really a functional shoe.' We went back and forth like that until I cracked her up and made her day so much that she just loved us!"

The Zappos purpose is to "live and deliver WOW."

In today's world, incorporating a social media strategy into the service mix is one way to ensure you're rolling out the red carpet and delivering WOW in every possible way.

Be Where Your Customers Are

Apryl DeLancey, president and CEO of Social Age Media, is proud to say that Byron Katie, author of a method of self-inquiry simply called "The Work," is one of its clients. "We assumed," says Apryl, "that her audience was mostly women over 35. However, upon completing an audit of everyone engaging on her social platforms, we discovered that her message was also resonating with young men and women between the ages of 18 and 30."

- ✓ At that point, Social Media Age staff changed Byron Katie's social media strategy, ensuring that Katie was found on a variety of platforms where the younger crowd is hanging, including Periscope Live Chats, Instagram, and Tumblr.
- ✓ They also went to work creating content that makes sense for those platforms. For instance, they recently posted video of the author's laughing granddaughter playing with her dog. DeLancey wisely advises, "That's how you stay relevant and engage the younger audience. You have to go where they go, and engage in ways they care about. Millennials—all audiences for that matter—love to peek behind the scenes of a big brand. It's authentic and makes you more accessible."

In less than a year, Social Media Age has been able to move the needle and increase Katie's community in that generation.

Online-to-Offline Events

DeLancey also suggests creating what she calls online-to-offline events.

✓ She hosted the "Branding for Women" event for the LAX Marriott, a Social Age Media client. Her staff put together a panel of experts and an exhibit hall for vendors and promoted it as a networking event using Event-Brite and social media outlets. The Marriott was able to showcase its property as *the* place to hold events or host out-of-town guests. The vendors were able to promote their own brands through sponsored prizes and booths. Attendees were able to learn from the experts and network with other community leaders. The hotel received 350 million impressions through social media and other online blogs. By partnering with others, they were able to keep the costs low and the return on investment (ROI) high.

Connect With Your Customers

Tampa-based social selling and social media trainer Phil Gerbyshak (*www.philgerbyshak.com*), shares these tips for connecting with your customers using a variety of platforms:

✓ Set up an Instagram account and share pictures of your customers, employees, and products. Encourage them to tag themselves and their friends in the pictures. Then respond to each one, and follow them and their friends.

✓ Share interviews with your customers, testimonials, and case studies on YouTube. Respond to each comment. Share the videos on all your other social channels and e-mail the links via your newsletter or your blog to give them maximum exposure.

✓ Create a hashtag for your business and post it on your social channels, in your newsletter, and on your receipts and invoices. Recognize those who use your hashtag with a thank you or shout-out. Be sure to monitor the hashtag and share relevant posts on your social channels, giving credit to the original poster. A great example of this is #Datz4Foodies.

✓ Respond to all customer inquiries quickly. If they are complaints, take them offline to fix them, and then go back online to give thanks for the opportunity to make things right. Everyone makes mistakes. What matters is how quickly—and how genuinely—you recover.

✓ *Never* blame the customer for a mistake, even if he or she is in the wrong. You will wind up looking petty and defensive at best, and wrong at worst. People will look for ways to make you look bad if you make them look bad.

✓ Find out what the most important days are in the eyes of your customers and recognize them on social media. This could be their birthday, anniversary, date of the birth of their first child, or a company celebration. Whatever it is, give them a shout-out on social media.

✓ Bonus points for holding a monthly party (virtual or in person) to celebrate customer special events. With permission, take pictures or videos using Zoom.us or Eyejot or YouTube. Capture and post to all your social networks.

✓ Be sure to let your customers know you'll be sharing on social media, and where, so they can look for themselves and share with their family and friends.

Other quick social media tips

✓ Rick Salmeron of Salmeron Financial likes to use his Facebook page to extend the client experience beyond the borders of his office. Rather than post dry statistics or boring financial articles, he uses his page to give customers a window into the soul of the company. He shares photos of what's going on in the office or posts humorous photos and fun trivia. "We're the financial planning company with personality!" says Rick.

✓ Partner with people in your community who are extremely active on social media. For instance, Asheville Community Theatre provides free opening-night tickets to local social media mavens. They are called Tweet Seats, and the recipients are set up and encouraged to tweet during the show.

✓ The community theatre also has fun with its fans, encouraging patrons to post videos on subjects related to its current production on its Facebook page. One popular invitation asked audience members to post their version of the famous Marlon Brando "Stella!" cry, when the theater was producing *A Streetcar Named Desire*.

✓ Hillary Kokajko and Lyndsey Derrow of High Point University consistently monitor what's being said on social media about the university and are very responsive. If there's an issue that needs to be addressed, they'll pick up the phone or meet with the student face-to-face and resolve it. If someone is pro-HPU online, they'll often send the person a little surprise such as some university swag.

✓ Shel Horowitz, coauthor of *Guerilla Marketing to Heal the World: Combining Principles and Profit to Create the World*

We Want (Morgan James Publishing, March 2016), uses social media to connect with celebrities who might help by reviewing and endorsing his books and products. Says Horowitz, "You retweet their tweets. You comment on their Facebook posts and blogs, and send them fan mail when they write something in their newsletter that particularly resonates with you. In other words, you simply interact with them online, one human being to another."

✓ The marketing team at Garden Spot Village Retirement Community, led by Scott Miller, uses a variety of social platforms to increase customer and prospect engagement, including YouTube. They use the video sharing Website to post reviews of their community and events and show videos of resident events. They even produce a show called *Endeavors*, hosted by Miller himself, which highlights the upcoming happenings at Garden Spot Village.

✓ Have you run across a social vending machine full of Pepsi products? In addition to purchasing your own soft drink, the machine prompts you to buy a Pepsi for a friend or perform a "random act of refreshment" by sending one to a stranger.

✓ Rita Tateel is the president and founder of Celebrity Source, a service that matches companies, brands, and organizations with celebrities to make appearances, endorse their product, or speak at their event. You may remember her from my first book, *The Celebrity Experience: Insider Secrets to Delivering Red Carpet Customer Service*. Says Rita, "It's no secret that celebrities are some of the strongest influencers in today's society. People live vicariously through the lives of celebrities and fantasize about what they could also have in their own lives, including the products and services to which celebrities are connected. Our society wants to be them, and when we can't, we at least want to be like them."

Rita suggests using the combined power of Hollywood and sports stars and video to position your product and services, and give your customers a little celebrity experience of their own. Says Rita, "Video is the fastest-growing visual communication method. In fact, online video production will account for more than one-third of all online advertising spending in the next five years." Rita has provided small to mid-sized businesses a way to have well-known celebrities endorse them through her VideoDorsements program. Rita presents customers with a list of celebrities to choose from, works with the stars to ensure they are comfortable with the company or product, and sets up one-day shoots for multiple clients to keep the costs low. It's an innovative way to use the power of celebrity to build credibility and buzz about your company. You can learn more at *www.TheCelebritySource.com*.

Mainstream Media

Here are a couple of terrific ways people have used the mainstream media—namely television and radio—to engage their customers:

✓ Darlene Tenes is a television personality and the founder of Casa Q, a San Jose-based Hispanic lifestyle company, dedicated to providing unique products, services, and content geared toward people who embrace the Latino culture. For eight years, she hosted a "Best Darn Tamale Contest," through a local NBC affiliate station. Says Darlene, "We tasted tamales from everywhere and a mixture of cultures including Cajun, Latino, Guatemalan, and Peruvian. We even had local and national tamale makers."

The contest began as a three-minute segment. As interest continued to grow, it became a half-hour show. Through it, Tenes was able to promote her ornaments and other products while engaging her customers and growing her fan base.

✓ Angel Tuccy and Eric Reamer are the cohosts of *Experience Pros Radio Show*, billed as the most positive business talk-show in America. They were recently awarded The Best Morning Radio Show in Denver by Colorado Community Media. Perhaps one reason is because of their segment called "Fan Braggin' Friday." Says Angel, "There are consumer advocate shows where, if you have an issue with a company, you can call to complain and the show will seek a resolution for you. Part of our mission at *Experience Pros Radio Show* is to create a revolution in the way people treat business. We wanted to create a venue where people could rave and brag about companies who offer great customer service." On Fridays, they open up their phone lines for people to call in with good customer service stories. "Many times," says Angel, "the experiences aren't earth shattering. They are often something simple, such as, "They carried my groceries out to the car because it was rainy and they saw I had a baby and toddler in tow." It turns out it's the littlest things that make people feel valued. Truly, when you hear or read the stories, it's just simple kindness. It's been really overwhelming to see how an act of kindness can have such an impact on somebody's world."

✓ Tuccy and Reamer began Fan Braggin' Friday in 1999 by encouraging 100 of their friends to call in with a good customer-service story. Though it took a while to catch on, now the phones ring off the hook and people wait on hold for 20 minutes to get through to tell their story. When a company has been "fan-bragged" about, the cohosts send them a postcard to let them know. "It's fun to feature our local businesses in a way that no one else is," exclaims Angel. Of course, although they are based in Denver, they are open to fan-brags from anywhere. If you have a story to share, you may want to call 855-FAN-BRAG on a Friday morning, or follow the Twitter hashtag #FanBrag to read even more great customer service stories.

Following are some other ways organizations are building the buzz about their businesses through unique marketing ideas and customer experiences.

Once You've Lost Your Virginity

Remember The Village Coffee Shop and the round of applause you get when you're found out as a "Village Virgin"?

- ✓ Once you've lost your "virginity," you're given a Village V Card. (Ask your teenager to explain it to you.) Instead of getting points for ordering meals, you earn them by bringing in Village Virgins. Introduce three new guests to the restaurant and you are treated to a half-order of French toast. "And we have the best French toast," adds owner Shanna Henkel. Another three new guests gets you a free pancake. Two more and you can order whatever entrée you'd like, on the house.
- ✓ However, it's the granddaddy prize that has regulars combing their contact lists for prospective customers. It's a T-shirt "so special, we refuse to sell it for money," comments Shanna. The only way to earn it is to bring in 10 Village Virgins. "People get so excited about this," says

Shanna. "We started the program a handful of years ago and have given away well over 200 T-shirts." This, of course, translates into more than 2,000 new customers!

Garden Spot Village Marathon

If there's anyone who understands the impact of experience marketing, it's Scott Miller, chief marketing officer for Garden Spot Village in New Holland, Pennsylvania. Not content to rely on traditional means of advertising the senior living community, Scott and his team consistently come up with fresh ideas to roll out the red carpet—inside and outside their walls.

✓ For instance, if you find yourself in Lancaster County in April 2016, consider running the eighth annual Garden Spot Village Marathon. Scott ran a marathon himself in 2008. Then he began looking for one that was held locally. No luck! So, he pitched the idea of sponsoring a marathon in New Holland to the Garden Spot leadership team. They said yes. Scott laughs as he admits, "We had no idea what we were getting into."

Even so, they often receive e-mails from people stating, "It's one of the most well-organized marathons we've ever participated in!" Of course, they have a built-in team of 300 resident volunteers who come out to ensure it's a special day for the runners. Says Scott, "It's a way to extend hospitality, invite people onto our campus, and give everyone involved a great experience!"

The event began in 2009 with 380 runners made up of Garden Spot Village residents and employees, as well as people from the outside community. Last year, they attracted 1,500 runners from all over the country. The event includes a full marathon, a half marathon, and a newly added kids' marathon. Children are on the honor system to run 25 miles before the day of the race and then run the last 1.2 miles on the campus during the event. They are treated to the entire race experience including T-shirts, medals, hats, pasta dinners, and recovery.

The Garden Spot Village marathon has provided the organization with name recognition in the local community. It brings people of all ages in huge numbers to their campus to engage and participate. Incidentally, the average age that most people move into a senior living center is 82. At Garden Spot Village, most new residents are in their early 60s.

✓ The campus also serves as the spot for "Pedal to Preserve," a fundraising cyclist event sponsored by the Lancaster Farmland Trust. This provides Scott with another opportunity to showcase Garden Spot Village in front of another 1,500 or more people.

✓ Anytime you provide a red-carpet experience for kids and their grandparents, you know you have a winner! If you're a resident of Garden Spot Village, and you have grandkids, you probably spend all year looking forward to the annual "Grand and Kids Camp." It's a week-long adventure with a variety of activities and events. It gives the older adults quality time with their grandchildren without their having to organize anything. It's all planned for them. In 2015, for example, the theme was "recycling." The campers toured a landfill site and a paper recycling plant, where they had a blast tearing books apart and throwing them into the bin.

✓ They also attend picnics, go tubing, and participate in a variety of projects together. When one young camper's parents tried to plan a family vacation on the same dates, he simply stated, "Those dates will have to change or I'm not going. I'm going to 'Grand and Kids camp!'"

✓ Before they leave the area, attendants take a ride on the Garden Spot Village hot air balloon. Owned and operated by USA Hot Air Balloon, it displays the logo of GSP for all to see. It's open for business on their campus. Residents and staff members especially enjoy their 20-percent discount!

The Red-Carpet Realtor

When Sheryl Simon became the fourth broker to list a high-end luxury home in Weston, Massachusetts, she knew she would have to pull a rabbit out of her hat and do something extraordinary to give this property a bigger presence. The 16-million-dollar home had been on the market (with other realtors) for over three years. Sheryl would have to refresh it and give it new positive energy. When a friend mentioned that she wanted to do a fundraiser for an organization that financially helped disadvantaged women and children, she had an idea.

✓ Sheryl approached the homeowner about hosting the fundraiser in his home. Aside from giving the seller renewed exposure, it was for a great cause! Sheryl used her connections to secure donations of liquor, flowers, and food. She gained commitments from celebrity guests. The music was provided by a DJ, who donated his time. A local car dealership donated some very elaborate cars. It became a true, red-carpet event, complete with a literal red carpet. The fundraiser attracted 250 guests and gained an incredible amount of media exposure. They raised $12,000.00 for the charity, and the house sold three weeks later. Says Sheryl, "For me, real estate is always [about] thinking outside the box because there are many people who take ordinary actions. It's all about what you bring to the party and what kind of extraordinary energy and service you provide."

✓ Sheryl also believes it's important to treat *all* customers like stars. For the last 23 years she's been giving catered open houses, complete with delicious food, for real estate brokers. They are held at the home of a realtor's client, with the hope that the brokers will then show the listed home to their buyers. Most are done for high-end homes. However, says Sheryl, "I like to treat every listing like it's high-end. I don't care if it's a 16-million-dollar home or one selling for $300,000.

✓ Whenever Sheryl is at a new listing, she's also tweeting and blogging about it. So she's getting the information out there and keeping her name in front of people at the same time.

✓ Sheryl once brought together all the people she sold to in the previous year and treated them to a lobster fest. She also hosted a party for a client who had just moved into a new neighborhood, in his new backyard. "I invited everyone who lived nearby. It was a great way for my client to meet his new neighbors!"

✓ Sometimes, Sheryl will run random contests for prizes. For instance, she's purchased gift certificates for a local restaurant and gifted them to the first three people to e-mail her to request them. "This makes my job more fun! We're in a very, very competitive business, and I see so many people doing the same old, same old. It doesn't work anymore. I spend money on my business and it comes back tenfold. It's not just about the immediate commission, but it's about having that phone ring and hearing that one of my past customers told the person on the other end that *you just have to work with Sheryl!* When they've entrusted me with their close friends and colleagues, then I know I've done a great job!"

Culture Conference

✓ The team at Pronexia is based in Quebec, Canada. They bill themselves as new generation headhunters. One strategy they use to make long-lasting impressions on their customers is to host annual, high-end, invitation-only events. These have ranged from fully catered cocktail parties to exclusive conferences at which they bring in industry experts to speak on a variety of topics. Says cofounder Marina Byezhanova, "We ensure our clients receive full VIP treatment throughout each event. It has helped us solidify our relationships with them."

✓ One such event, held in June 2015, focused on the topic of company culture. They booked top-notch speakers, provided meals and beverages—including fresh organic juices and a coffee bar—and gave each guest a gift basket. Marina adds, "The amount of raving feedback we received in the weeks that followed was overwhelming. Whereas we used to devote significant resources to extending invitations to these events, our clients now look forward to them and follow up proactively to find out about the next one." She asks, "What better way to maintain client relationships than to impress them so much that it entices to them to reach out to your sales team instead of the other way around?"

Family Movie Night

✓ Realtor Alex Bracke is based in Northern Virginia. He is the number-one agent in his brokerage, with millions of dollars in annual sales. Alex has several client appreciation gatherings each year. But the biggest and most anticipated event is his annual family movie day. Says Alex, "We rent out a movie theater for a day and show a family-friendly movie. In 2015, we showed Pixar's *Home*." Apropos, considering his business! In addition to free tickets to the movie, families are given free popcorn. They walk down a red carpet as they arrive and have their photos taken in front of a special background. "It's as if they are the stars of the show," enthuses Alex. While families are watching the movie, the photos are developed, framed, and handed out as parting gifts when the movie is over.

Surprise Dinner Party

✓ Aegis FinServ Corp is a diverse financial services company that operates in three spaces: banking, business payroll/rewards/gift debit cards, and business intelligence consulting. Most of their clients intertwine and cross paths, and many know each other personally. Once a year, the company holds an appreciation event called the AegisFS Surprise Dinner Party. Jim Angleton, president of Aegis FinServ Corp shares the details:

> We invite 30 couples, representing owners or executives of each customer company to meet at an obscure location, such as the parking lot of a golf course. I greet and welcome everyone as they mill about in an

air-conditioned tent, which houses a full bar and can-apé selections. When everyone has arrived, we roll out a large board with thirty envelopes tacked to it. Each couple takes one envelope and opens it. Inside the envelope is a card with the number of a car. We open the curtains dramatically to reveal the limos lined up waiting. Each couple boards their limo by number. There are six people per car. Inside, they enjoy a goodie bag filled with a *Sunday Miami Herald* paper [The event is always on Saturday night], nice champagne, two freshly baked chocolate croissants, a bag of Jamaican Blue Mountain coffee beans, and a little handwritten note expressing our gratitude for their patronage. Each limo goes to an unnamed top-ten restaurant in Miami. The drivers are sworn to secrecy until they arrive. The customers are greeted by the owners and chefs of each restaurant. They enter to enjoy an eight-course meal. I stop by every restaurant to say hello [and] ensure they are enjoying the food and having fun! Once the meal is over, they get back in their limos to conclude the evening at the starting location. This event costs exactly the same as [going] to an exclusive country club and [hiring] a band. But it is fun and unique. Our clients love it!

Shoes for the Needy

Dr. Daniel Margolin, owner of New Jersey Foot and Ankle Center in Oradell, New Jersey, knows that sometimes red-carpet service means just giving back to the community.

✓ That's why the podiatrist and his team created their "Shoes for the Needy" campaign. "I began to notice that many of my patients with foot problems would talk about having to put their brand new shoes aside because they no longer fit," explains Dr. Dan. He asked them, "What did you do with them?" Most people were just throwing them away.

✓ So Dr. Dan and his team put up a few posters in the office asking people to bring in the shoes they were throwing away so they could donate them to people in need. The small internal campaign exploded. Within a year or two, they had been given 15,000 pairs of shoes. They've been running the campaign for more than 27 years. Although they get more shoes on some years than others, they consistently receive 10,000 or more pairs a year for charity. Some are donated by corporations, but most come from individual patients.

Although it was not his original intention, Dr. Margolin and his practice have certainly earned some media exposure through the effort. It's the moments like the following story that keep him going:

It's pretty rare that people will actually come to our office for shoes. Most of the time, we give them to local charity groups. However, sometimes, people will come in and ask for them. One day, I was in the office and a gentleman came in and told me his son had just gotten out of prison. He was finally able to land a job in construction but he needed work boots. He was a big kid who needed a men's size 13: "We just don't have the money to buy them and I was hoping you'd have some that would fit the bill." The chances of me having a size 13 men's work boot is about zero, but let's go back and take a look. The guy comes in with me. I open the door and, I swear to God, they were right there. It was like a light was beaming down on this pair of Garrett size 13 work boots! I handed them to the man and he hugged me and started crying. It was one of those moments where you know that, sometimes, you do something because the payment for them is simply the fact that it touches another human being in some way. If, after all the years of doing this campaign, that was the only thing I got out of it, then it was just awesome. It was just an awesome experience.

The "Shoes for the Needy" campaign runs from September to March every year.

✓ The team at New Jersey Foot and Ankle Center also hosts a "Patient Appreciation Week" at least once a year. For one such event, they invited Steve Weatherford, a former punter for the New York Giants, to come to the office. "He's such a good guy," says Dr. Dan. "We had over 150 people in the office, and he spent hours posing for photos and signing autographs." During the events they hold drawings and give away lottery tickets, and everyone gets gift cards for donuts. "We make it a whole week, so it's a pretty festive time in the office."

Seven-Star Events

Ruby Newell-Legner is a fan experience expert, an international speaker, an author, and the founder of *www.7StarService.com*. The 2015/2016 president of the National Speakers Association has worked with hundreds of professional sports teams, organizations, professional associations, and agencies to help them create legendary fan experiences and increase customer loyalty and retention. Here she shares some of the tips she gives her clients on how to roll out the red carpet before, during, and after an appreciation event for loyal customers:

✓ "When it comes to guest or customer appreciation events, focus only on showing your gratitude rather than on getting them to sign on the dotted line. Be clear about the reason for the event. Make sure every staff member, partner, and entertainer in the audience understands the goal.

✓ Ask yourselves, 'Once the event is over, what needs to happen for us to feel the event was a success?'

✓ Consider each element of the event and identify specific steps you'll take at each touch point to make each guest feel special.

✓ Create a custom invitation that someone might feel proud to display prominently on his/her desk.

✓ Handwrite addresses on the envelopes for a more personalized approach.

✓ Mail invitations at least six weeks in advance to ensure invitees can easily put your event on their schedule.

✓ Be sure to request an RSVP. When they call to confirm their attendance, say, 'We have only invited our most loyal fans and we are excited you will be joining us.'

✓ When they arrive for your event, call them by name and let them know you've been expecting them.

✓ Provide nametags that say something like 'Season Ticket Holder Since 1976' or 'Loyal customer since 2002.' Or you could personalize nametags with guests' hometowns, hobbies, years of service, or nicknames.

✓ Assign hosts to specific guests who will connect with those people as soon as they arrive, for a more personalized welcome.

✓ Make sure you wrap up the event with a fond farewell and a sincere 'thank you for coming' as they leave.

✓ Personally hand each guest a 'thank you for attending' gift. Make it something that is congruent with the event and that your guests will appreciate.

✓ Follow up with each attendee by personal phone call or email.

✓ Debrief with the entire team after the event so your next one is even better."

Partnerships and Pairings

✓ Yet another way that Celebration! Cinema builds buzz and partners with businesses in the local community is through its "Brewed for Film" series. The company has partnered with a local brewery called Founders. For a 10-week time period it shows classic films and offers appropriate beer pairings. Says Emily Loeks, "We played *Shaun of the Dead* and paired it with Pale Ale. We played *The Graduate* and served a Porter. You get the idea. They have a beer called Dirty Bastard and we paired it with *Dirty Rotten Scoundrels.* We want to help people have an experience in the theater that they can't have watching a movie at home. If you ask people about a film experience they had as a child, it's often a story about going to a movie with Grandma, or going to see *Star Wars* with a huge number of people who were dressed up and in the lines. We try to do things at Celebration! Cinema to [make] those kinds of experiences happen."

✓ They also have a program called "Sensory Showtimes" that enables individuals with autism and other similar conditions to comfortably enjoy a movie experience with their friends and family. They keep the lights in the auditorium up higher and turn down the volume so it's less jarring.

Says Emily, "We offer programming like that to enable people to have a good experience with each other. They love the fact that they have a place where they can enjoy a movie as a family and not be divided up. It's wonderful not only for the child with special needs, but for their siblings, parents, and friends as well."

When it comes to building buzz about your business, nowadays it's about creating stories worth sharing. Whether it's through your social media channels, the hosting of special events, or contribution to the community, giving customers an insider view of your organization gives them something to talk about.

Questions for Discussion

- How could we better use social media to engage our customers?
- What type of events would engage and show appreciation for our customers?
- How could we improve our level of community involvement?

CHAPTER EIGHT

Step Over the Velvet Rope

In 2012, one of my dreams came true. My cousin Liam, who was selected to sit in the bleacher seats on the red-carpet for the Academy Awards, invited me to join him. The experience was better than I ever could have imagined! We were seated hours early and I sat enthralled, watching the media and others bustle about as they prepared for the arrival of the celebrities. The red carpet itself was divided in half by a velvet rope. On one side of the velvet rope sat the fans, or the "bleacher creatures," as we called ourselves, as well as people attending the ceremony who were not doing the press junket. On the other side of the velvet rope were the media, the celebrity wranglers and, eventually, the celebrities themselves.

Finally the moment we all had been waiting for arrived. The celebrities began to appear. Octavia Spencer, Gwyneth Paltrow, and Jessica Chastain were red-carpet ready in their gorgeous gowns. Stephen Spielberg and Tony Bennett looked dashing in their tuxes. They all gave us a great experience. As fans shouted out each celebrity's name, they would turn and wave at the bleachers, smile, blow kisses, and pose long enough for us to get a good photo. This is all we wanted. We are, after all, their "customers." We're the people who go see their movies.

One celebrity went above and beyond. That man was George Clooney. Whenever possible, Mr. Clooney stepped *over* the velvet rope and engaged with fans, signing autographs, posing for photos with people, and clowning around. To my knowledge, he was the only celebrity who did that. He was also the one *everyone* talked about after the red-carpet experience. In fact, even today, on a private Facebook page, my fellow "bleacher creatures" will remark, "Remember how great George Clooney was?" I'm sure you can see where I'm going with this. It's this kind of service that will get your customers buzzing about your business. You must be willing to "step over the velvet rope" and engage your customers in a way that your competition won't. You must be committed to doing a little bit extra, always. Applying some of the ideas in this book will help you do this. Whether you are a solo entrepreneur, the manager of a small business or mid-sized company, or a vice president in a large corporation, I hope you have found in this book many useful ideas that will help you step over the velvet rope and roll out the red carpet for your customers.

Maybe you're swimming in ideas and don't know where to start. Why don't you start with a planning session? Gather your team for 15 minutes every day for the next 31 days. If you're a solo entrepreneur, find a quiet place to do some thinking by yourself or invite input from colleagues and friends. Get yourself a journal and write down your thoughts and action ideas as you implement your 31-day plan of action. Doing the following exercise will help kick-your journey of customer service improvement:

1. Be a detective. As you do business today, notice the service you *receive* as you visit other organizations. Notice the *feelings* you have during each interaction.

2. Identify each point of contact you have with a customer during your day-to-day interactions. Include your Website, phone conversations, and face-to-face engagement. Make a list of all the places and times when you are able to impact a customer.

3. List the feelings you want your customer to have at each point of engagement.

4. List the tangible, actionable service behaviors that can create those emotions.

5. Have someone "secret shop" your company. As you hear or read his or her feedback, notice the gap between your vision of red-carpet service and the reality of what your customers are likely experiencing.

6. Take all the ideas you've highlighted and the answers to the questions you've discussed and write your compelling vision for red-carpet customer service. What do you want your customer experience to look like, sound like, feel like?

7. Decide how you will measure the success of your customer-service improvement journey.

8. Lead by example. Pay attention to where your own behavior matches your vision for service excellence, and where there is room for improvement.

9. Identify areas of your infrastructure that may need to change in order to provide the needed foundation for extraordinary service.

10. Choose one idea for making red-carpet first impressions. Whether it's an idea taken directly from this book or something you've come up with on your own, implement it in your organization.

11. Discuss ideas for making red-carpet last impressions. Decide when you will implement your favorite idea in your organization.

12. Decide what you will do from this point forward to ensure you're hiring people who have the talents needed to deliver on your expectations and do a great job.

13. Discuss or think about where you most need to become red-carpet ready.

14. Identify the skills you and/or your team members need in order to deliver on your service vision.

15. Identify resources for educating yourself and/or your team.

16. Take one step toward becoming red-carpet ready.

17. Make a list of 10 of your best customers or referral sources.

18. Find out as much as you can about those 10 people in terms of favorites and preferences and enter this information into your customer management system.

19. Choose a customer or two and practice making "movie moments."

20. Decide on a method for collecting and processing customer feedback.

21. Outline a process for responding to negative comments or reviews. How will you turn an unhappy customer into a happy customer?

22. Call three customers today just to surprise them. Thank them for being customers and ask them for their honest feedback.

23. Re-read Chapter 6.

24. Choose one idea you will implement tomorrow to roll out the red carpet for your team members. If you don't have employees, consider the people who mentor, champion, and assist you on your journey.

25. Implement the idea you decided on yesterday.

26. Choose one thing you will do to better engage with your customers using social media.

27. Brainstorm events you could produce to show appreciation for your customers.

28. Think about a way your organization could better serve the larger community.

29. Discuss what it means to step over the velvet rope in your organization.

30. Solidify your plan of action with the top five ideas you are going to implement immediately.

31. Finally, the most important step of all: begin.

When I visited Mather LifeWays a few years ago, I asked Gale Morgan to tell me why the company had been able to implement so many amazing red-carpet ideas when so many other similar companies were struggling to do so. Here's what she told me:

✓ "We take one idea at a time and decide to implement.

✓ We have all the logistical discussions we need to have in order to implement [each idea].

✓ Invariably there is push-back. We don't give up. We keep the conversation going until we have a system.

✓ Once the idea is systemized, we execute a few times and refine it.

✓ Before you know it, we can't remember a time when we weren't rolling out the *orange* carpet in that way."

That's the key! You see, most of us give up when the conversations get tough. Those who excel don't stop the conversation until they have a solid system in place. Remember: all red-carpet organizations have this in common: They never settle for status quo. Go back and read about Mather LifeWays; G Adventures; Davinci; High Point University; Sheryl Simon; Rick Salmeron of Salmeron Financial. Revisit Talent

Plus; The Hotel at Auburn University; Celebration! Cinema; Mama D's; and Northwell Health. These and so many others are filled with people who are on a constant mission to up their game, and create a culture that empowers everyone on their team (big and small) to roll out the red carpet for their customers. You can do the same.

It's worth it. When you do, you'll experience the *thrill* of the red carpet.

Where your customer matters.

Your work matters.

And you matter.

And that, ladies and gentlemen, is a wrap!

The End

INDEX

ABOUT THE AUTHOR

When she was a little girl, Donna excitedly watched her mother and grandmother roll out the red carpet to welcome family members home—just as if they were stars of the silver screen. Today Donna Cutting helps you experience the thrill of the red carpet, where your customer matters, your work matters, and *you* matter.

Cutting is the founder and CEO of Red-Carpet Learning Systems, Inc., a consulting firm that offers tools and training to help leaders engage their teams to deliver world-class customer service. Her client list includes healthcare, senior living, entertainment, retail, and banking professionals who want to turn prospects into customers and customers into raving fans. She and her team help them create a service culture in which the entire workforce becomes an engaged and integral part of their sales force by focusing on customer delight.

Donna is also a popular inspirational keynote speaker, whose experience as an actress sets the stage for her high-energy, theatrical, and comedic speaking style. An active member of the National Speakers Association, she is a certified speaking professional, a designation held by less than 15 percent of professional speakers worldwide.

She's also the author of *The Celebrity Experience: Insider Secrets to Delivering Red Carpet Customer Service* (Wiley, 2008), and has published many articles online and in trade publications. She's been quoted in print publications, such as *Investors' Business Daily*, and appeared on a variety of television and radio shows. Her blog can be found on her Website: *www.redcarpetlearning.com.*

Donna makes her home in the beautiful mountains of Asheville, North Carolina, with her husband, Jim, and their rescue dogs, Moxie and Tonks.

––––––––––

Donna and the team at Red-Carpet Learning Systems, Inc., would like to know what *you're* doing to roll out the red carpet for your customers. Share your story with us and you could be featured on our blog and in Donna's next book. Have you spied a red carpet customer service superstar out there? Snap his/her photo and nominate him/her for the Red Carpet Service Hall of Fame by sending the photo and story to Red-Carpet Learning Systems, Inc.

Donna's contact information:

Donna@RedCarpetLearning.com.

Red-Carpet Learning Systems, Inc.

PO Box 19798

Asheville, NC 28815

(800) 519-0434

www.redcarpetlearning.com

Like us on Facebook at: *http://facebook.com/donnacutting.*

Follow Donna on Twitter: @donnacutting.

Subscribe to our YouTube channel: *https://www.youtube.com/channel/UCP919IeaXhdrcXyEjPfvoHw.*

For inquires about speaking, training, and media appearances, please email us at Service@RedCarpetLearning.com.